Nick Vandome

iPhone
for Seniors

for all iPhones with iOS 12
illustrated using iPhone XR, XS and XS Max

In easy steps is an imprint of In Easy Steps Limited
16 Hamilton Terrace · Holly Walk · Leamington Spa
Warwickshire · United Kingdom · CV32 4LY
www.ineasysteps.com

Notice of Liability
Every effort has been made to ensure that this book contains accurate
and current information. However, In Easy Steps Limited and the
author shall not be liable for any loss or damage suffered by readers
as a result of any information contained herein.

Trademarks
iPhone® is a registered trademark of Apple Computer, Inc. All other
trademarks are acknowledged as belonging to their respective
companies.

In Easy Steps Limited supports The Forest Stewardship Council (FSC),
the leading international forest certification organization. All our titles
that are printed on Greenpeace approved FSC certified paper carry the
FSC logo.

MIX
Paper from
responsible sources
FSC® C020837

Printed and bound in the United Kingdom

ISBN 978-1-84078-834-1

Contents

1 Your New iPhone 7

2 Starting to use your iPhone 29

1 Your New iPhone

The iPhone is a sleek, stylish smartphone that is ideal for anyone, of any age. This chapter introduces the three models of the iPhone, and takes you through its buttons and controls. It also shows how to set it up, ready for use.

This latest range of iPhones has no Home button (for the first time since the iPhone was launched). The functions that were previously undertaken by the Home button are now done by a range of gestures on the screen, and by using the buttons on the body of the iPhone. See pages 16-18 for details about these gestures. For older iPhones that have a physical Home button and run iOS 12, the relevant commands will also be listed throughout the book.

The New icon pictured above indicates a new or enhanced feature introduced with the iPhone XR, XS and XS Max, or the latest version of its operating system, iOS 12.

Hands on with the iPhone

The iPhone is one of the great success stories of the digital age. It is one of the world's leading smartphones: a touchscreen phone that can be used for not only making calls and sending text messages, but also for online access and a huge range of tasks through the use of apps. Essentially, the iPhone is a powerful, compact computer that can be used for everything you need in your mobile life.

The latest range of iPhones includes the iPhone XS and XS Max, and the iPhone XR. All models use the iOS 12 operating system, and the A12 Bionic chip processor.

iPhone XR

This is an upgrade to the previous standard range of iPhone; e.g. the iPhone 8. Its specifications include:

- **Screen**: The iPhone XR has a **6.1 inch** (measured diagonally) Liquid Retina HD display screen.

- **Storage**: This determines how much content you can store on your iPhone. For the iPhone XR, the storage capacity options are: 64GB, 128GB or 256GB.

- **Camera**. A 12-megapixel (MP) camera for taking photos, and a front-facing 7MP TrueDepth camera for taking self-portraits (selfies) and for use with Face ID.

- **Face ID**. Unlock the iPhone by looking at the screen.

- **Battery power**: The iPhone XR provides up to 65 hours of wireless audio playback, 16 hours' video playback, 15 hours' internet use, and 25 hours' talk time on wireless.

- **Input/Output**: There is a Lightning Connector port (for charging, headphones, and connecting to a computer); a built-in speaker; and a built-in microphone.

- **Water resistant.** Water resistant up to 1 meter for 30 minutes. Also splash- and dust-resistant.

- **Sensors**: The sensors are: accelerometer, barometer, ambient light sensor, proximity sensor, and gyroscope.

iPhone XS

This is the second generation of the revolutionary iPhone X that was released in 2017. Its specifications include:

- **Screen**: The iPhone XS has a **5.8 inch** (measured diagonally) Super Retina HD display screen.

- **Storage**: This determines how much content you can store on your iPhone. For the iPhone XS, the storage capacity options are: 64GB, 256GB or 512GB.

- **Camera**. A dual lens 12-megapixel (MP) camera for taking photos, and a front-facing 7MP TrueDepth camera for taking self-portraits (selfies) and for use with Face ID.

- **Face ID**. Unlock the iPhone by looking at the screen.

- **Battery power**: The iPhone XS provides up to 60 hours of wireless audio playback, 14 hours' video playback, 12 hours' internet use, and 20 hours' talk time on wireless.

- **Input/Output**: These are a Lightning Connector port (for charging, headphones and connecting to a computer), built-in speaker and a built-in microphone.

- **Water resistant.** Water resistant up to 2 meters for 30 minutes. Also splash- and dust-resistant.

- **Sensors**: The sensors are: accelerometer, barometer, ambient light sensor, proximity sensor, and gyroscope.

Beware

The amount of storage you need may change once you have bought your iPhone. If possible, buy a version with as much storage as your budget allows.

Don't forget

Face ID for unlocking the iPhone is now available on the full range of the latest iPhone models; i.e. iPhone XR, XS and XS Max. For details about setting this up, see page 24.

Don't forget

None of the latest range of iPhones has a separate headphone jack: this is accommodated using the Lightning Connector port.

...cont'd

Don't forget

All iPhone models have connectivity for fast 802.11ac Wi-Fi, 3G/4G, and Bluetooth 5.0.

Don't forget

All three of the latest iPhones can be connected to an High Definition (HD) TV with AirPlay Mirroring and an Apple TV box. This then displays whatever is on your iPhone on the TV screen.

Hot tip

To connect your iPhone to an HDTV you will need an Apple Lightning/Digital AV adapter, an Apple Lightning/VGA adapter, or an Apple Lightning/HDMI adapter (sold separately).

iPhone XS Max

This is a larger version of the iPhone XS, which has the largest screen of any iPhone to date. Its specifications include:

- **Screen**: The iPhone XS Max has a **6.5 inch** (measured diagonally) Super Retina HD display screen.

- **Storage**: This determines how much content you can store on your iPhone. The iPhone XS Max the storage capacity options are: 64GB, 256GB or 512GB.

- **Camera**. A dual lens 12-megapixel (MP) camera for taking photos, and a front-facing 7MP TrueDepth camera for taking self-portraits (selfies) and for use with Face ID.

- **Face ID**. Unlock the iPhone by looking at the screen.

- **Battery power**: The iPhone XS Max provides up to 65 hours of wireless audio playback, 15 hours' video playback, 13 hours' internet use, and 25 hours' talk time on wireless.

- **Input/Output**: These are a Lightning Connector port (for charging, headphones and connecting to a computer), built-in speaker and a built-in microphone.

- **Water resistant.** Water resistant up to 2 meters for 30 minutes. Also splash- and dust-resistant.

- **Sensors**: The sensors are: accelerometer, barometer, ambient light sensor, proximity sensor, and gyroscope.

What do you get?

The iPhone box contains all of the items required to use your new iPhone, charge it, and open the SIM tray to add a SIM card. The various components are:

- **iPhone**. The iPhone will be turned off, but there should be enough charge in the battery to turn it on without having to charge it first.

- **The Lightning to USB cable**. This can be used for charging the iPhone, or connecting it to a computer for downloading items.

- **The EarPods**. These can be used to listen to audio items on your iPhone. They can also be used to manage phone calls using the central control button (see page 56 for details). There is no headphone jack for the latest iPhone EarPods, as they connect via the Lightning Connector.

- **The SIM tool**. This is a small metal gadget that is in a cardboard envelope in the iPhone box. It is used to open the SIM tray so that a SIM card can be inserted (see pages 14-15 for details).

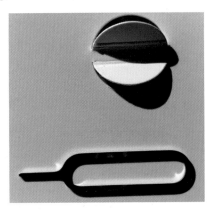

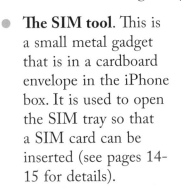

There is a wide range of accessories for the iPhone. These include cases in a range of colors and materials. These cases give some protection to the body of your iPhone.

To charge your iPhone with the Lightning to USB cable: insert the Lightning Connector into the bottom of the iPhone, and insert the USB connector into the plug that is also provided in the iPhone box. Connect the plug to a socket to charge your iPhone.

The latest iPhones support wireless charging, by placing the device on a compatible base station.

iPhone Nuts and Bolts

For more details on turning on the iPhone, see page 16.

The iPhone XR comes in a range of colors: Black, Blue, Coral, White, Yellow and Red. The iPhone XS and XS Max come in Gold, Space Gray and Silver.

To make phone calls with your iPhone you need to have an active SIM card inserted, and a suitable service provider for cellular (mobile) calls and data. The iPhone XR, XS, and XS Max use a nano SIM card, which is smaller than both the standard size and the micro size.

On/Off (Side) button

The button for turning the iPhone On and Off (and putting it into Sleep mode) is located on the top right-hand side of the body (looking at the screen). As with other buttons on the body, it is slightly raised to make it easier to locate just by touch.

Volume controls

Volume is controlled using two separate buttons on the left-hand side of the body. They do not have symbols on them but they are used to increase and decrease the volume.

Ringer/silent (use this to turn the ringer On or Off for when a call or a notification is received)

Volume up

Volume down

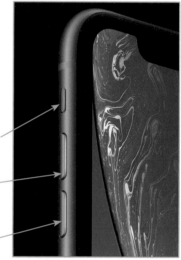

Top notch

All iPhones have a notch at the top of the screen that accommodates the TrueDepth camera, sensors for use with Face ID, built-in stereo speakers, and a built-in microphone.

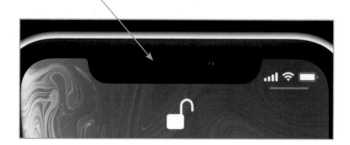

12

Lightning Connector, speakers and microphone
These are located at the bottom of the iPhone.

Stereo speakers

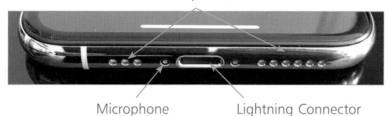

Microphone   Lightning Connector

Back view of the iPhone
This contains the main camera, the LED flash, and the rear microphone. The iPhone XR and XS/XS Max have slightly different back views.

iPhone XR

Main camera

Rear microphone   LED flash (and torch)

iPhone XS/XS Max

The iPhone XS and XS Max have two lenses for the main camera: one wide-angle and one telephoto. They combine to take each shot. The LED flash (and flashlight/torch) is in between the two camera lenses.

Don't forget

The main camera on all iPhone models is a high-quality 12-megapixel camera. It can capture excellent photos and also 4K (ultra-high definition) and high definition (HD) video. The front-facing TrueDepth camera has a 7-megapixel resolution and can be used for taking "selfies"; the modern craze of taking a photo of yourself and then posting it online on a social media site such as Facebook. It is also used for the Face ID functionality for unlocking the iPhone (see page 24), and for FaceTime video calls (see pages 118-119).

13

Inserting the SIM

The SIM card for the iPhone will be provided by your mobile carrier; i.e. the company that provides your cellular phone and data services. Without this, you would still be able to communicate with your iPhone, but only via Wi-Fi and compatible services. A SIM card gives you access to a mobile network too. Some iPhones come with the SIM pre-installed, but you can also insert one yourself. To do this:

Don't forget

The phone services for the iPhone are provided by companies that enable access to their mobile networks, which you will be able to use for phone calls, texts, and mobile data for access to the internet. Companies provide different packages: you can buy the iPhone for a reduced sum and then pay a monthly contract; typically for 12 or 24 months. Despite the fact that the initial outlay for the iPhone will be cheaper, this works out more expensive over the period of the contract. Another option is to buy the iPhone (make sure it is unlocked so that you can use any SIM card) and use a SIM-only offer. This way, you can buy a package that suits you for calls, texts and mobile data. Look for offers that have unlimited data for internet access.

1 Take the SIM tool out of the iPhone box and remove it from its cardboard packaging

2 Insert the SIM tool into the small hole on the SIM slot on the side of the iPhone

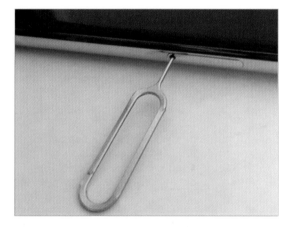

3 Press the tool firmly into the hole so that the SIM tray pops out and starts to appear. Pull the SIM tray fully out

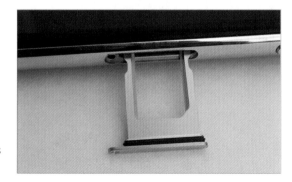

4 Place the SIM card with the metal contacts face downwards (shown facing upwards in the image). Place the SIM tray in position so that the diagonal cut is in the same position as the cut on the SIM card

Hot tip

If you lose the SIM tool you can use the end of a stretched-out paper clip instead.

5 Place the SIM card into the SIM tray. It should fit flush, resting on a narrow ridge underneath it, with the diagonal cut on the card matching the cut in the tray

6 Place your thumb over the bottom of the SIM tray, covering the SIM card, and place the tray into the SIM slot, with the metal contacts facing the back of the phone. Push the tray firmly into the slot until it clicks into place

Beware

The SIM tray can only be inserted in one way. If it appears to encounter resistance, do not force it; take it out and try again. The hole in the SIM tray should be nearest to the bottom of the phone body.

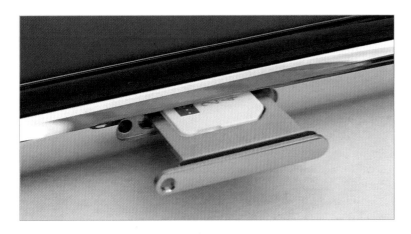

Don't forget

For older iPhones that have a physical Home button and run iOS 12, some of the functionality on these three pages is achieved with the Home button. These instances will be noted throughout the book.

Hot tip

If your iPhone ever freezes, or if something is not working properly, it can be rebooted by pressing the Volume Up button, then the Volume Down button, then pressing and holding the On/Off button.

Beware

The color of the bar at the bottom of the screen, for returning to the Home screen, is dependent on the background color of the app being used. If it has a light background, the bar will be a dark color; if it has a dark background the bar will be a light color.

iPhone Gestures

Since none of the new models of iPhone have a Home button, all off the actions that were previously accessed by pressing the Home button have been replaced by gestures on the screen and actions using the On/Off and Volume buttons. Gestures for the iPhone include the following (also including some general iPhone actions):

Turning on

Press and hold on the On/Off button for a few seconds. Keep it pressed until the Apple icon appears. This will display the Lock screen (see below).

Unlocking the iPhone

This is done by using Face ID. Once this has been set up (see pages 24-25), raise the phone so that the camera can view your face, and simultaneously swipe up from the bottom of the screen.

Returning to the Home screen

Swipe up from the bar at the bottom of the screen. This can be done from any app.

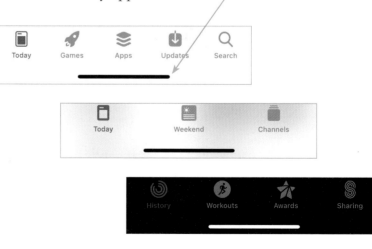

Accessing the Control Center

To access the Control Center of useful widgets, swipe down from the top right-hand corner of the screen. (On older models of iPhone, this was achieved by swiping up from the bottom of the screen, which now returns you to the Home screen.)

Buy a glass screen protector to help preserve your iPhone's screen. This will help prevent marks and scratches, and can also save the screen if it is broken: the protector breaks rather than the iPhone's screen itself.

Accessing the Notification Center

The Notification Center is accessed by swiping down from the top left-hand corner or the middle of the screen.

Accessing Siri

Press and hold the On/Off button until Siri appears. Alternatively, use the Hey Siri function (see pages 38-39).

Accessing the App Switcher

Swipe up from the bottom of the screen and pause in the middle of the screen to view open and recently-used apps.

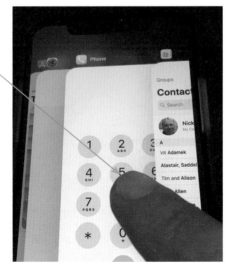

The methods of accessing the Control Center, Siri, and the App Switcher are all new features on the latest range of iPhones with iOS 12.

...cont'd

Reachability

To use Reachability, which moves the items on the screen to the bottom half, to make them easier to access with one hand, swipe down from the bottom of the screen (see page 44 for more details).

Taking a screenshot

To capture an image of what is currently on the screen, quickly press and release the On/Off button and the Volume Up button simultaneously. For older iPhones that have a physical Home button and run iOS 12, a screenshot can be captured by pressing the On/Off button and the Home button simultaneously.

Paying with Apple Pay

To use Apple Pay to pay for items with your iPhone, double-click the On/Off button, and authorize with Face ID. See pages 54-55 for details about setting up Apple Pay.

Turning off

Press and hold the On/Off button and either of the volume buttons until the Power Off screen appears. Swipe the **slide to power off** button to the right to turn off the iPhone.

Screenshots are saved to the **Photos** app. They can be viewed here from the **Photos** button on the bottom toolbar and also the **Screenshots** album in the **Albums** section.

For older iPhones that have a physical Home button and run iOS 12, press and hold the On/Off button and access the **slide to power off** button.

Getting Set Up

When you first turn on your iPhone there will be a series of setup screens. These include the following options:

- **Language**. Select the language you want to use.

- **Country**. Select the country in which you are located.

- **Quick Start**. This can be used to transfer settings from another compatible iOS device.

- **Wi-Fi network**. Connect to the internet, using either your own home network or a public Wi-Fi hotspot.

- **Data & Privacy**. This is used to identify features that ask for your personal information.

- **Face ID.** Use this to create a Face ID for unlocking your iPhone by looking at it while swiping up from the bottom of the screen. See page 24 for details.

- **Create Passcode**. This can be used to create a numerical passcode for unlocking your iPhone.

- **Apps & Data**. This can be used to set up an iPhone from an iCloud backup, or as a new iPhone.

- **Apple ID and iCloud**. This can be used to use an existing iCloud account or to create a new one.

- **Keep your iPhone Up to Date**. This can be used to install updates to the operating system (iOS) automatically.

- **Location Services**. This determines whether your iPhone can use your geographical location for apps.

- **Siri.** This can be used to set up Siri, the digital voice assistant, ready for use.

- **Screen Time**. This can be used to set limits for using apps on the iPhone and for creating a usage report.

- **iPhone and App Analytics**. This allows details from the iPhone and its apps to be sent to Apple and developers.

Most of the options available during the setup process can also be accessed within the **Settings** app.

For more information about using iCloud, see Chapter 3.

Screen Time is a new feature in iOS 12.

iPhone Settings

The Settings app controls settings for the way the iPhone and its apps operate:

The Cellular (Mobile) Data settings contain the **Data Roaming** option (**Cellular > Cellular Data Options**): if you are traveling abroad you may want to turn this **Off** to avoid undue charges for when you are connected to the internet. If in doubt, contact your provider before you go.

To change the iPhone's wallpaper, tap once on the **Choose a New Wallpaper** option in the **Wallpaper** setting. From here, you can select system images, or ones that you have taken yourself and saved on your iPhone.

- **Apple ID, iCloud, iTunes & App Store**. Contains settings for these items.

- **Airplane Mode**. This can be used to disable network connectivity while on an airplane.

- **Wi-Fi**. This enables you to select a wireless network.

- **Bluetooth**. Turn this On to connect Bluetooth devices.

- **Cellular (Mobile) Data**. These are the settings that will be used with your cellular (mobile) service provider.

- **Personal Hotspot**. This can be used to share your internet connection.

- **Notifications**. This determines how the Notification Center operates (see pages 26-27).

- **Sounds & Haptics**. This has options for setting sounds for alerts and actions such as tapping on the keyboard.

- **Do Not Disturb**. Use this to specify times when you do not want to receive audio alerts, phone calls, and video calls.

- **Screen Time**. Options for reporting on and limiting iPhone usage.

- **General**. This contains a range of common settings.

- **Control Center**. This determines how the Control Center operates (see pages 34-37).

- **Display & Brightness**. This can be used to set the screen brightness, text size, and bold text.

- **Wallpaper**. This can be used to select a wallpaper.

- **Siri & Search**. Options for the digital voice assistant.

- **Face ID & Passcode**. This has options for adding a passcode or fingerprint ID for unlocking the iPhone.

- **Emergency SOS.** This can be used to set an Auto Call to an emergency number.

- **Battery**. This can be used to view battery usage by apps.

- **Privacy**. This can be used to activate Location Services so that your location can be used by specific apps.

- **iTunes & App Store**. This can be used to specify downloading options for the iTunes and App Stores.

- **Wallet & Apple Pay**. This can be used to add credit or debit cards for use with Apple Pay (see pages 54-55).

- **Passwords & Accounts.** This contains options for managing website passwords and adding online accounts.

- **Mail**, **Contacts**, **Calendars**. These are three separate settings that have options for how these apps operate.

- **Notes**. This has formatting options for the Notes app.

- **Reminders**. This has an option for syncing reminders.

- **Voice Memos**. Options for recording voice memos.

- **Phone**. Settings for making calls (see pages 72-73).

- **Messages**. Options for how the Messages app operates.

- **FaceTime**. This is used to turn video calling On or Off.

- **Maps**. This has options for map distances and map type.

- **Measure**. Options for setting the unit of measurement.

- **Safari**. Settings for the default iPhone web browser.

- **News**. Settings for specifying access for the News app.

- **Stocks**. Privacy settings for the Stocks app.

- **Camera**. This has options for the camera's operation.

- **Music**, **Videos**, **Photos**, **Books**, and **Podcasts**. Settings for how these five apps manage and display content.

If a Settings option has an On/Off button next to it, this can be changed by swiping the button to either the left or right. Green indicates that the option is **On**. Select **Settings** > **General** > **Accessibility** > **On/Off Labels** to show or hide the icons on each button.

Tap on a link to see additional options:

DISPLAY ZOOM	
View	Standard >

Tap once here to move back to the previous page for the selected setting:

‹ Settings   **Display & Brightness**

BRIGHTNESS

21

iOS 12 is a new feature introduced with the iPhone XR, XS and XS Max. It can also be used on all iPhones that could run iOS 11.

You will need an Apple ID for all Apple online services. This is free – to register go to **https://appleid.apple. com**

Tap on **Create Your Apple ID**. You will be prompted to enter your email address and a password. Then follow the on-screen instructions. Tap on **Create Apple ID** when ready.

To check the version of the iOS, look in **Settings** > **General** > **Software Update**.

About iOS 12

iOS 12 is the latest version of the operating system for Apple's mobile devices including the iPhone, the iPhone and the iPod Touch.

iOS 12 further enhances the user experience for which the mobile operating system is renowned. This includes:

- **Performance**. iOS 12 is not such an immediately obvious update as previous versions, in terms of the user interface and new features. However, a lot of the improvements are aimed at better performance in a number of areas: faster app launching, faster access to the keyboard, faster camera launching, and prolonged battery life. These changes may not always be immediately obvious, but they will help improve the overall performance of your iPhone with iOS 12.

- **Screen Time**. Monitoring usage of mobile devices is becoming an increasing concern, both for ourselves and younger uses. In iOS 12 the Screen Time function enables users to set limits for using specific apps or functions, and provides an overview of how much the user is using the device and also a weekly report.

- **Siri Shortcuts**. In iOS 12 it is possible to create a sequence of events such as getting directions to a destination, sending a text message, and setting a smart thermostat in the home, all with a single Siri command.

- **New app**. The Measure app is a new app on the iPhone, and it can be used to measure straight surfaces.

- **Updated apps**. Several apps have been given an overhaul in iOS 12, including: the Apple Books app, which is renamed from the iBooks app and has a new interface; the News app has been redesigned so that it is easier to access new content; and the Photos app has a new For You tab for your favorite photos, memories, and albums, and an improved search facility.

Using the Lock Screen

To save power, it is possible to set your iPhone screen to auto-lock. This is the equivalent of the Sleep option on a traditional computer. To do this:

1 Tap once on the **Settings** app

2 Tap once on the **Display & Brightness** tab

> AA Display & Brightness

3 Tap once on the **Auto-Lock** option

> Auto-Lock   Never >

4 Tap once on the time of non-use after which you wish the screen to be locked

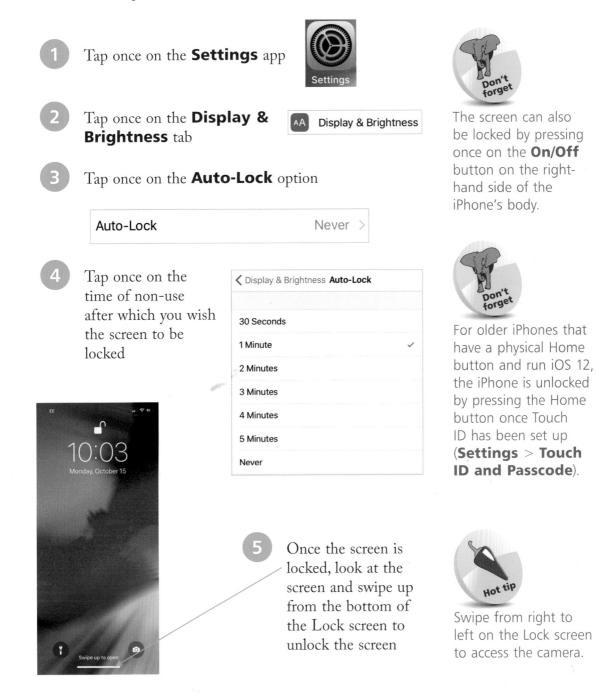

> ‹ Display & Brightness **Auto-Lock**
>
> 30 Seconds
> 1 Minute   ✓
> 2 Minutes
> 3 Minutes
> 4 Minutes
> 5 Minutes
> Never

5 Once the screen is locked, look at the screen and swipe up from the bottom of the Lock screen to unlock the screen

---

Don't forget

The screen can also be locked by pressing once on the **On/Off** button on the right-hand side of the iPhone's body.

Don't forget

For older iPhones that have a physical Home button and run iOS 12, the iPhone is unlocked by pressing the Home button once Touch ID has been set up (**Settings** > **Touch ID and Passcode**).

Hot tip

Swipe from right to left on the Lock screen to access the camera.

Face ID and Passcode

With the removal of the Home button on the latest range of iPhones, the means of unlocking the phone is done through the use of Face ID. If this cannot be used for any reason, a passcode can be entered instead. To set up Face ID:

Hot tip

Face ID can also be used for contactless purchases for Apple Pay (see pages 54-55), and purchases in the iTunes and App Store. Drag the buttons **On** as required under the **Use Face ID For** heading in the **Face ID & Passcode** settings.

1 Select **Settings** > **Face ID & Passcode**

2 Tap once on the **Set Up Face ID** button

3 Position your face in the center of the circle that accesses the iPhone's camera. Move your head slowly in a circle so that the camera can record all elements of your face

Don't forget

For older iPhones that have a physical Home button and run iOS 12, the Touch ID feature is used, rather than Face ID (**Settings** > **Touch ID and Passcode**).

4 Tap once on the **Continue** button after the first scan. A second scan will be done to complete the process

5 Tap once on the **Done** button to finish the Face ID setup process

Adding a passcode

If Face ID cannot be used to unlock the iPhone, a numerical passcode can be used instead. This has to be set up at the same time as creating a Face ID. To do this:

1 Select **Settings** > **Face ID & Passcode**

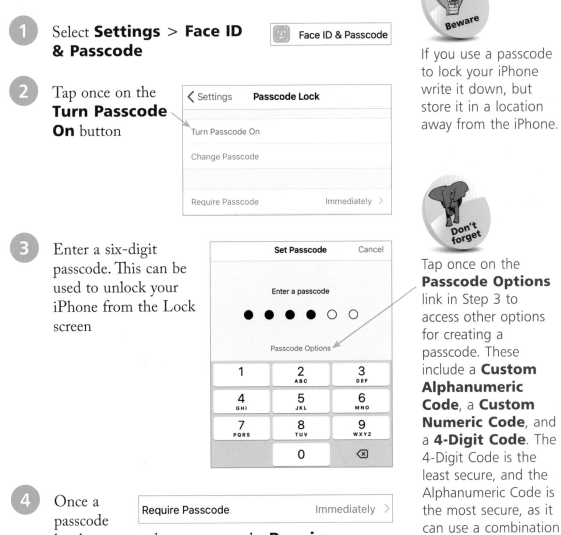

| :) | Face ID & Passcode |

Beware

If you use a passcode to lock your iPhone write it down, but store it in a location away from the iPhone.

2 Tap once on the **Turn Passcode On** button

‹ Settings	**Passcode Lock**
Turn Passcode On	
Change Passcode	
Require Passcode	Immediately ›

3 Enter a six-digit passcode. This can be used to unlock your iPhone from the Lock screen

Set Passcode	Cancel

Enter a passcode

● ● ● ● ○ ○

Passcode Options

1	2 ABC	3 DEF
4 GHI	5 JKL	6 MNO
7 PQRS	8 TUV	9 WXYZ
	0	⌫

Don't forget

Tap once on the **Passcode Options** link in Step 3 to access other options for creating a passcode. These include a **Custom Alphanumeric Code**, a **Custom Numeric Code**, and a **4-Digit Code**. The 4-Digit Code is the least secure, and the Alphanumeric Code is the most secure, as it can use a combination of numbers, letters and symbols.

4 Once a passcode

Require Passcode	Immediately ›

has been created, tap once on the **Require Passcode** button in Step 2 to specify a time period until the passcode is required on the Lock screen. The best option is **Immediately**, otherwise someone else could access your iPhone

Notifications

Notifications can be used with iOS 12 so that you never miss an important message or update. Notifications can be viewed in the Notification Center and also on the Lock screen. To set up and use Notifications:

Hot tip

The Notification Center can be accessed by dragging down from the top left-hand corner or the middle of the screen, in any app.

Hot tip

Turn the **Lock Screen** option to **On** in Step 4 to enable notifications for the selected app to be displayed even when the iPhone is locked.

Hot tip

Text messages can be replied to directly from the Lock screen, without unlocking the iPhone. To do this, press on the message on the Lock screen and compose a reply as normal.

1 Tap once on the **Settings** app

2 Tap once on the **Notifications** tab

3 Under **Notification Style**, tap once on an item to select the notification settings for a specific app

4 Drag the **Allow Notifications** button to **On** to display notifications from this app in the Notification Center

5 Tap here to select the style for how the notification appears

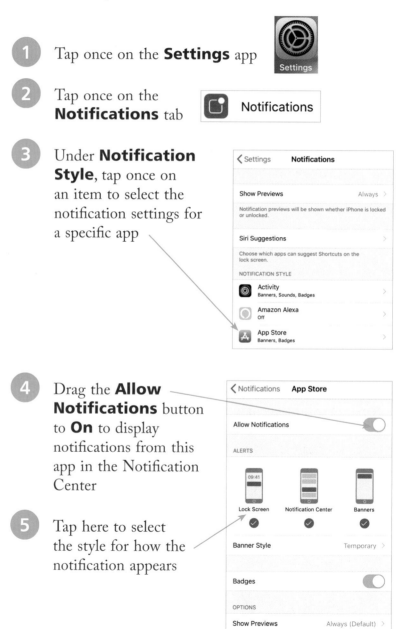

6 Swipe down from the top left or middle of the iPhone screen, from the Home screen or any app, to view your notifications in the Notification Center. This is split into two sections: the notifications page, which contains notifications from the apps in Step 3 opposite; and the widgets page that contains widgets with real-time information about topics such as the weather, stocks, and news; the Up Next calendar item; and notifications from the apps. Swipe right and left to move between the two pages

The items in Step 6 can also be viewed directly on the Lock screen. Swipe left and right to view the two separate screens. The notifications page can also be viewed from the Home screen by swiping from left to right.

 7 Swipe to the bottom of the widgets page, and tap once on the **Edit** button to manage the widgets that appear here. Tap on a red circle to delete a widget from the Today page, or scroll down and tap on a green button to add a new widget

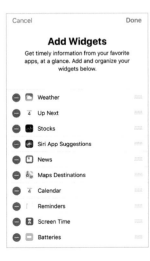

At the bottom of the window in Step 5 on the previous page there is a **Notification Grouping** option. Set this to **Automatic**, so that all similar notifications are grouped together. This is a new feature in iOS 12.

27

Updating Software

The operating system that powers the iPhone is known as iOS. This is a mobile computing operating system, and it is also used on the iPad and the iPod Touch. The latest version is iOS 12. Periodically there are updates to the iOS to fix bugs and add new features. These can be downloaded to your iPhone once they are released:

Hot tip

It is always worth updating the iOS to keep up-to-date with fixes. Also, app developers update their products to use the latest iOS features.

1 Tap once on the **Settings** app

2 Tap once on the **General** tab
(a red tag indicates that an update is available)

| ⚙ | General | | ① | › |

3 Tap once on the **Software Update** option

| | Software Update | | ① | › |

Software Update can be set to be performed automatically overnight, when the iPhone is charging and connected to Wi-Fi. Tap on the **Automatic Updates** button in Step 4 and drag the **Automatic Updates** button to On. This is a new feature in iOS 12.

4 If there is an update available it will be displayed here, with details of what is contained within it

5 Tap once on the **Download and Install** button to start the downloading process. The iOS update will then be done automatically

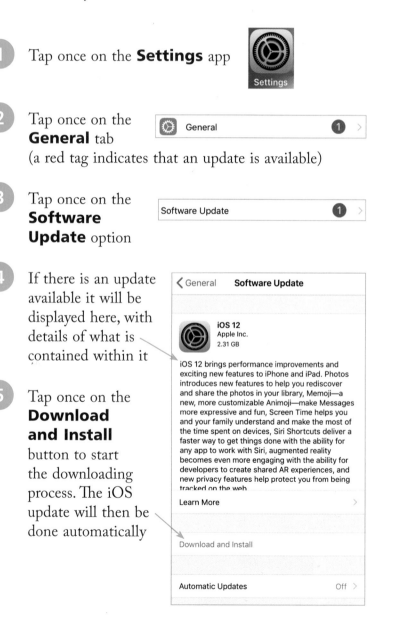

‹ General   **Software Update**

iOS 12
Apple Inc.
2.31 GB

iOS 12 brings performance improvements and exciting new features to iPhone and iPad. Photos introduces new features to help you rediscover and share the photos in your library, Memoji—a new, more customizable Animoji—make Messages more expressive and fun, Screen Time helps you and your family understand and make the most of the time spent on devices, Siri Shortcuts deliver a faster way to get things done with the ability for any app to work with Siri, augmented reality becomes even more engaging with the ability for developers to create shared AR experiences, and new privacy features help protect you from being tracked on the web.

Learn More   ›

Download and Install

Automatic Updates   Off ›

Automatic Updates ⬤

28

2 Starting to use your iPhone

This chapter covers the functions on the iPhone that you need to use it confidently and make the most of its features. From opening and closing apps, using Screen Time to monitor your iPhone usage, and using Apple Pay, it explains the iPhone environment so you can quickly get up and running with it.

Opening and Closing Items

All apps on your iPhone can be opened with the minimum of fuss and effort:

1 Tap once on an icon to open the app

2 The app opens at its Home screen

3 Swipe up from the bottom of the screen to return to the iPhone Home screen. Swipe up from the bottom of the screen and pause in the middle of the screen to access the App Switcher

Don't forget

When you switch from one app to another, the first one stays open in the background. You can go back to it by accessing it from the App Switcher window or the Home screen.

Don't forget

For older iPhones that have a physical Home button and run iOS 12, press the Home button to return to the Home screen. To access the App Switcher, double-click the Home button.

4 From the App Switcher window, swipe left and right between open apps, and tap on one to make it the active app. Swipe an app to the top of the window in the App Switcher to close it

Navigating Around

The iPhone screen is very receptive to touch, and this is the main method of navigating around, through a combination of swiping, tapping, and pinching.

Swiping between Home screens
Once you have added more apps to your iPhone, they will start to fill up more Home screens. To move between these:

 Swipe left or right with one or two fingers to move between Home screens

In addition to swiping between two screens there are a combination of tapping, swiping, and pinching gestures that can be used to view items such as web pages, photos, maps, and documents, and also to navigate around the iPhone.

Swiping up and down
Swipe up and down with one finger to move up or down web pages, photos, maps or documents. The content moves in the opposite direction of the swipe; i.e. if you swipe up, the page will move down, and vice versa.

Tapping and zooming
Double-tap with one finger to zoom in on a web page, photo, map or document. Double-tap with one finger to return to the original view.

Pinching and swiping
Swipe outwards with thumb and forefinger to zoom in on a web page, photo, map or document.

Pinch together with thumb and forefinger to zoom back out on a web page, photo, map or document.

You can also move between different screens by tapping once on the small white dots in the middle of the screen above the Dock (see page 32).

The faster you swipe on the screen, the faster the screen moves up or down.

Swiping outwards with thumb and forefinger enables you to zoom in on an item to a greater degree than double-tapping with one finger.

Using the Dock

By default, there are four apps on the Dock at the bottom of the iPhone's screen. These are the four that Apple thinks you will use most frequently:

- **Phone**, for making and receiving calls.

- **Safari**, for web browsing.

- **Messages**, for text messaging.

- **Music**.

You can rearrange the order in which the Dock apps appear:

With iOS 12, some of the pre-installed apps can be deleted from your iPhone. These are indicated by a cross in the top left-hand corner when you press and hold on an app, as in Step 1.

 Press and hold on one of the Dock apps until it starts to jiggle

Just above the Dock is a line of small white dots. These indicate how many screens of content there are on the iPhone. Tap on one of the dots to go to that screen.

 Drag the app into its new position

 Swipe up from the bottom of the screen to exit editing mode

Adding and removing Dock apps

You can also remove apps from the Dock and add new ones:

 To remove an app from the Dock, press and hold it, and drag it onto the main screen area

If items are removed from the Dock they are still available in the same way from the main screen.

 To add an app to the Dock, press and hold it, and drag it onto the Dock

Editing mode can also be exited by tapping on the **Done** button in the top right-hand corner of the screen.

 The number of items that can be added to the Dock is restricted to a maximum of four, as the icons do not resize

For older iPhones that have a physical Home button and run iOS 12, press the Home button to exit editing mode for the Dock

 Swipe up from the bottom of the screen to exit editing mode

Using the Control Center

The Control Center is a panel containing some of the most commonly-used options within the **Settings** app.

The method of accessing the Control Center is new for the latest models of iPhone using iOS 12.

Accessing the Control Center

The Control Center can be accessed with one swipe from any screen within iOS 12, and it can also be accessed from the Lock screen. To set this up:

1 Tap once on the **Settings** app

2 Tap once on the **Control Center** tab, and drag the **Access Within Apps** button On or Off to specify if the Control Center can be accessed from there (if it is Off, it can still be accessed from any Home screen)

AirDrop is the functionality for sharing items wirelessly between compatible devices. Tap once on the **AirDrop** button in the Control Center and specify whether you want to share with **Contacts Only** or **Everyone**. Once AirDrop is set up, you can use the **Share** button in compatible apps to share items such as photos with any other AirDrop users in the vicinity.

3 Swipe down from the top right-hand corner of any screen to access the Control Center

Control Center functionality

The Control Center contains items that have differing formats and functionality. To access these:

1 Press and hold on the folder of four icons in the top left-hand corner, to access the **Airplane Mode**, **Cellular Data**, **Wi-Fi**, **Bluetooth**, **AirDrop**, and **Personal Hotspot** options

2 Press on the **Music** button to expand the options for music controls, including playing or pausing items and changing the volume. Tap once on this icon to send music from your iPhone to other compatible devices, such as AirPod headphones or HomePods, Apple's wireless speakers

The Control Center cannot be disabled from being accessed from the Home screen.

3 Tap once on individual buttons to turn items On or Off (they change color depending on their state)

For older iPhones that have a physical Home button and run iOS 12, access the Control Center by swiping up from the bottom of the screen.

4 Drag on these items to increase or decrease the screen brightness and the volume

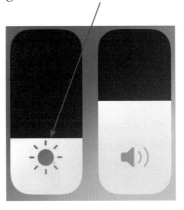

Hot tip

Bluetooth can be used to connect to other compatible devices, using radio waves over short distances up to approximately 20 meters. Both devices must have Bluetooth turned on and be "paired" with each other. This links them together so that content such as photos can be shared between them.

Don't forget

Press and hold on the Camera button to access options for taking a "selfie" (a self-portrait), recording a video, recording a slow-motion video, and taking a standard portrait.

...cont'd

Control Center controls

Access the items in the Control Center as follows:

- Tap once on this button to turn **Airplane mode** On or Off, for network connections.

- Tap once on this button to turn **Cellular Data** On or Off, for cellular networks.

- Tap once on this button to turn **Wi-Fi** On or Off.

- Tap once on this button to turn **Bluetooth** On or Off.

- Tap once on this button to activate **AirDrop** for sharing items with other AirDrop users.

- Tap once on this button to turn **Personal Hotspot** On or Off, to use your iPhone as a hotspot for connecting to the internet.

- Tap once on this button to **Lock** or **Unlock** screen rotation. If it is locked, the screen will not change when you change the orientation.

- Tap once on this button to turn **Do Not Disturb** mode On or Off.

- Tap once on this button to turn on the **Flashlight**. Press on the button to change the intensity of the flashlight.

- Tap once on this button to access the **Clock**, including a stopwatch and timer. Press on the button to access a scale for creating reminders.

- Tap once on this button to open the **Calculator** app.

- Tap once on this button to open the **Camera** app.

Customizing the Control Center

The Control Center can be customized so that items can be added or removed. To do this:

1 Tap once on the **Settings** app

2 Tap once on the **Control Center** tab

3 Tap once on the **Customize Controls** button

4 The items currently in the Control Center are shown at the top of the window; those that can be added are below them. Tap once on a red icon to remove an existing item, or tap once on a green icon to add new items to the Control Center

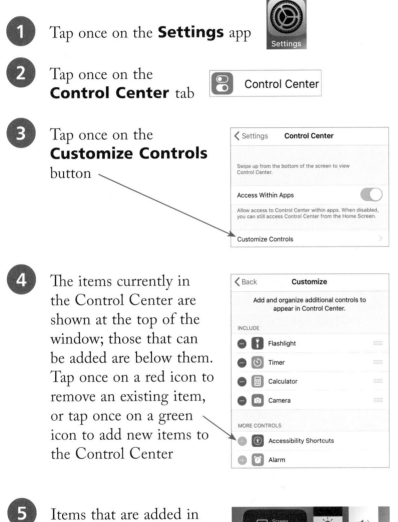

5 Items that are added in Step 4 are included in the Control Center, and can be accessed from here

Hot tip

The Flashlight and the Camera can both be accessed directly from the Lock screen too.

Setting up Siri

Siri is the iPhone's voice assistant that provides answers to a variety of verbal questions by looking at content in your iPhone and also web services. You can ask Siri questions relating to the apps on your iPhone, and also general questions such as weather conditions around the world or sports results. Initially, Siri can be set up within the **Settings** app:

Siri can be used to translate English words or phrases into different languages. More languages have been added in iOS 12, and there are now 50 different language pairs.

 Tap once on the **Settings** app

 Tap once on the **Siri & Search** tab

Options for Siri
Within the Siri settings there are options for its operation:

 Drag the **Listen for "Hey Siri"** button to **On** if you want to be able to access Siri just by saying **Hey Siri**

2 Make selections here for the language, voice type, feedback and your own details to use with Siri

‹ Settings	Siri & Search
ASK SIRI	
Listen for "Hey Siri"	⬤
Press Home for Siri	⬤
Allow Siri When Locked	⬤
Language	English (United States) ›
Siri Voice	American (Female) ›
Voice Feedback	Always ›
My Information	Nick Vandome ›

Siri can help you get things done just by asking. About Ask Siri & Privacy...

SIRI SUGGESTIONS	
Suggestions in Search	⬤
Suggestions in Look Up	⬤
Suggestions on Lock Screen	⬤

3 If using "Hey Siri", it has to be set up by training it for your voice. Tap once on the **Continue** button

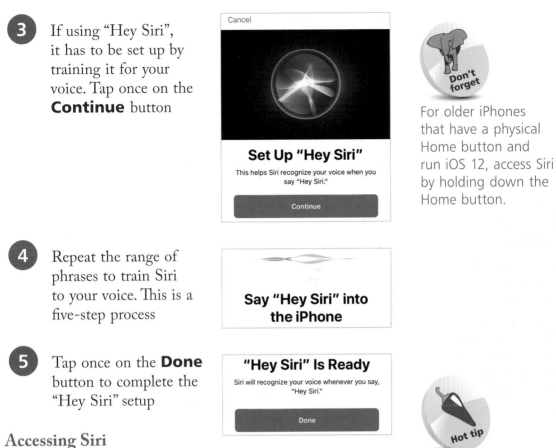

For older iPhones that have a physical Home button and run iOS 12, access Siri by holding down the Home button.

Cancel

Set Up "Hey Siri"

This helps Siri recognize your voice when you say "Hey Siri."

Continue

4 Repeat the range of phrases to train Siri to your voice. This is a five-step process

Say "Hey Siri" into the iPhone

5 Tap once on the **Done** button to complete the "Hey Siri" setup

"Hey Siri" Is Ready

Siri will recognize your voice whenever you say, "Hey Siri."

Done

Accessing Siri

There are two ways to access Siri (in addition to "Hey Siri"):

1 Press and hold the **On/Off** button until the Siri screen appears

2 Ask your question to Siri. After the reply, tap once on this icon to ask another question

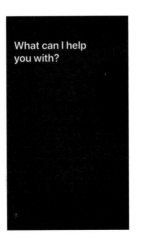

What can I help you with?

Siri can be used to open any of the pre-installed iPhone apps, simply by saying **Open Photos**, for example.

Finding Things with Siri

Siri is very versatile and can be used for a wide range of functions, including finding things on your iPhone, searching the web, getting weather forecasts, finding locations, and even playing music.

Accessing your apps

To use Siri to find things on your iPhone:

Hot tip

Siri can also display specific contacts. Say **Show me...** followed by the person's name to view their details (if they are in your contacts).

Hot tip

Siri can also read out your information: open an item such as calendar appointments and then say **Read appointment**.

Don't forget

You can ask for weather forecasts for specific periods such as **Today** or **This Week**. However, Siri's power of forecasting only stretches to 10 days in the future.

 Access Siri as shown on page 39

 To find something from your iPhone apps, ask a question such as **Open my contacts**

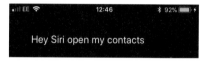

3 The requested app is displayed

Getting the weather

You can ask Siri for weather forecasts for locations around the world. Simply ask for the weather in a certain city or location.

Finding locations

Siri is also effective for viewing locations within the Maps app. This can be done on an international, national or city level. Siri can also be used to get directions.

Searching locally

If Location Services is turned On for Siri, then you can ask for local information such as **Show the nearest Indian restaurants**.

Playing music

You can use Siri to play any of the music that you have in the Music app. Simply ask Siri to play a track and it will start playing. (Music can be downloaded from the iTunes Store app; see page 150 for more details.)

To stop a song, simply say **Stop playing** and the song will be paused.

Siri can be used with certain third-party apps to perform tasks such as booking a taxi or a restaurant table.

Siri can also play a whole album as well as individual tracks.

Items can also be searched for using the Spotlight Search option. This can be accessed by swiping downwards on the Home screen and entering a keyword or phrase in the Search box at the top of the window. Items can be searched for on your iPhone (including apps), or use the **Search Web** button at the bottom of the window to search the web.

Siri Shortcuts is a new feature in iOS 12.

The available options in the Siri Shortcuts section are based on items that have previously been actioned and identified by Siri.

Shortcuts with Siri

Although Siri can be an invaluable companion in terms of finding information or accessing services, each request requires a separate interaction with Siri. One enhancement to this is being able to trigger an event, or sequence of events, with a single voice command. In iOS 12, this can be done through the use of Siri Shortcuts. Some single-event shortcuts are available in the Siri settings, and customized sequences can also be created with the Shortcuts app.

Siri Shortcuts

Existing shortcuts are available in the Siri settings:

 Open the Settings app and tap once on the **Siri & Search** option

 Topics for suggested shortcuts are listed on the Siri & Search page, based on actions that have already been performed

 Tap once on the **All Shortcuts** button to view all of the suggested items

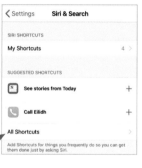

4 Tap once on one of the items to view its details

5 Tap once on the red **Record** button to record a voice command that will be used as a shortcut to trigger the action

6 The trigger word is displayed below the Siri command that it will activate

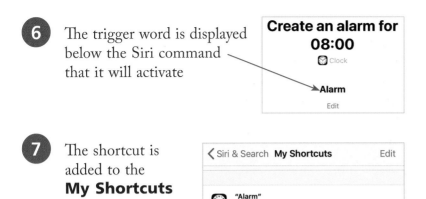

7 The shortcut is added to the **My Shortcuts** section that is accessed from the Siri & Search page

Using the Shortcuts app

Shortcuts in Siri can be created for actions that have already been undertaken. Using the Shortcuts app it is also possible to create new actions. To do this:

1 Download the **Shortcuts** app from the App Store and tap on it once to open it

2 Tap once on the **Create Shortcut** button

3 Suggested actions are listed in the bottom panel. Drag an action into the top panel to add it to the shortcut. Repeat this for each required action. These are the actions that will be performed when the shortcut is activated, using a trigger word as shown on the previous page

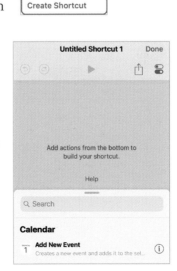

Hot tip

If you regularly phone the same people, create a shortcut for this, using a person's name as the trigger word for Siri. This can then be used to connect a call to them using a single word. To do this, make a call initially to a person manually, so that it will appear in the Suggested Shortcuts section.

Don't forget

Tap once on the **Done** button to create the completed shortcut.

Reachability

Because of the size of the iPhone XR, the iPhone XS, and the XS Max, it is not always easy to access all items with one hand. This is overcome by a feature known as Reachability, which can be accessed from any screen of the iPhone. This moves the items on the screen to the bottom half, and they can all be accessed from here.

The Reachability function is not turned on by default. To enable it, go to **Settings** > **General** > **Accessibility** and drag the **Reachability** button to **On**, underneath the **Interaction** heading.

For older iPhones that have a physical Home button and run iOS 12, access Reachability by gently double-tapping the Home button, rather than double-clicking.

The **Display & Brightness** settings can also be used to increase the text size for supported apps. Tap once on the **Text Size** button to access a slider with which you can set the required text size.

 By default, all items on the screen take up the whole area

2 Swipe down on the bottom edge of the screen

3 The items on the top half of the screen are moved to the bottom half

4 The Reachability effect stays in place for one action; e.g. after you tap on an item, the screen reverts to normal size

Night Shift

Getting a good night's sleep is becoming increasingly recognized as a vital and often overlooked element of our overall health and wellbeing. One of the biggest obstacles to this is the amount of artificial lighting that we experience at night time, such as street lighting, lighting in the home, and the light emitted from mobile devices such as iPhones. This type of light is known as "blue light", and it is one of the most restrictive in terms of getting a good night's sleep, as it is the type of light that instructs the body that it is time to be awake and alert. One option to reduce the impact of blue light from your iPhone is to use the Night Shift option, which reduces the amount of blue light that is emitted.

Beware

Try not to use your iPhone, or other mobile devices, for prolonged periods just before you go to bed, to reduce the amount of artificial light that you are experiencing. Also, it is best to turn off your iPhone when you go to bed, as it is a good way to suggest to your brain that it is time for sleep.

1. Tap once on the **Settings** app

2. Tap once on the **Display & Brightness** tab

   AA Display & Brightness

3. Tap once on the **Night Shift** button

   Night Shift   Off >

4. Drag the **Scheduled** button to **On** and tap once on the **From/To** option to set a time period for when Night Shift is applied

5. Tap once on the **Sunset to Sunrise** option to have Night Shift applied for this period

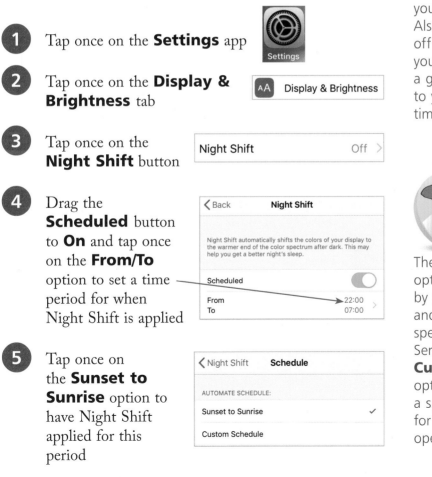

Don't forget

The Sunset to Sunrise option is determined by your iPhone's clock and its location as specified by Location Services. Tap on the **Custom Schedule** option in Step 5 to set a specific time period for when Night Shift operates.

The Do Not Disturb options have been enhanced in iOS 12.

Tap once on the **From/To** option in Step 4 to set the time period for Do Not Disturb.

The Bedtime option in Step 5 can be specified in the **Clock** app. Tap on the **Bedtime** button on the bottom toolbar and enter a time period that constitutes bedtime. The Clock app can be set to activate an alarm at the end of the bedtime period and Do Not Disturb will apply during the bedtime hours.

Do Not Disturb

The iPhone is excellent for keeping up-to-date with calls and notifications from apps, so you never miss an important call or message. However, there can be times when constant notifications can be too intrusive, and you may wish to have a period of quiet without having to turn off notifications completely. This can be achieved with the Do Not Disturb feature. To use this:

1 Tap once on the **Settings** app

2 Tap once on the **Do Not Disturb** tab

3 Drag the **Do Not Disturb** button to **On** to activate **Do Not Disturb**, so that calls and notifications will be muted

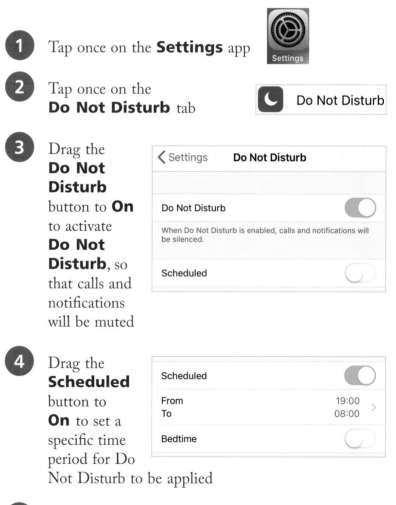

4 Drag the **Scheduled** button to **On** to set a specific time period for Do Not Disturb to be applied

5 Drag the **Bedtime** button to **On** to apply Do Not Disturb for these times (see the Hot tip)

Using 3D Touch

One of the features using touch on the iPhone is 3D Touch. This can be used to activate different options for certain apps, depending on the strength with which you press on an item. For instance, a single press or tap can be used to open an app. However, if you press harder on the app then different options appear. This can be used for Quick Actions, and Peek and Pop.

Quick Actions

The process for accessing Quick Actions with 3D Touch is the same for all compatible apps (this is for the Camera):

 Press deeper into the **Camera** app to access options for taking a selfie, recording a video, scanning a product code, or taking a regular portrait

Peek and Pop

3D Touch can also be used to view items within apps, with a single press. This is known as Peek and Pop. To use this, with the Mail app:

 Press on an email in your Inbox to peek at it; i.e. view it with the other items blurred out

2 Press deeper on the email to pop it open; i.e. view it in Preview mode, rather than opening it fully. (Swipe up on the Preview screen to access a menu for options for the email; e.g. Reply etc.)

3 Press deeper again on the email to open it fully in the Mail app and access its full functionality

Hot tip

Accessing the 3D Touch features requires specific extra pressure; it is not just a case of pressing with the same amount of pressure for a longer time. This is known as pressing "deeper" into an app. This also provides a slight buzzing vibration, known as haptic feedback.

Don't forget

Other apps that offer Peek and Pop include: Safari, Maps, Camera, and Photos. Items for Safari and Maps can be peeked at and accessed from within an email; e.g. if there is a website link in an email, press it once to view a preview of the web page, and press deeper to open it in Safari. Photos can be peeked at from the Camera app by pressing on a thumbnail image and then pressing deeper to open it.

Screen Time

The amount of time that we spend on our digital devices is a growing issue in society, and steps are being taken to let us see exactly how much time we are spending looking at our cellular phone screen. In iOS 12, a range of screen-use options can be monitored with the Screen Time feature. To use this:

Screen Time is a new feature in iOS 12.

1 Select **Settings** > **Screen Time**

 Screen Time

2 Tap once on the **Turn On Screen Time** button

‹ Settings	**Screen Time**
Turn On Screen Time	
Get a weekly report with insights about your screen time and set time limits for apps you want to manage.	

3 Options for using Screen Time are displayed

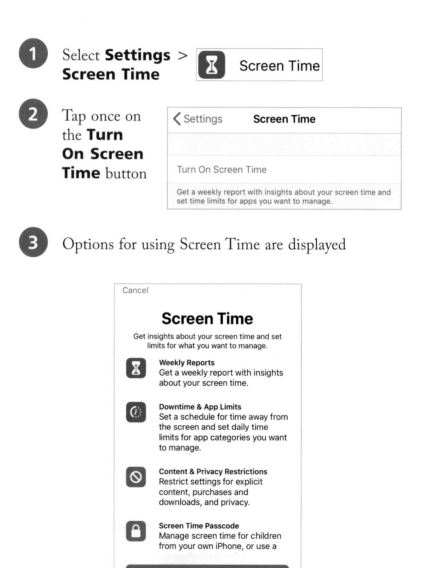

Cancel

Screen Time

Get insights about your screen time and set limits for what you want to manage.

Weekly Reports
Get a weekly report with insights about your screen time.

Downtime & App Limits
Set a schedule for time away from the screen and set daily time limits for app categories you want to manage.

Content & Privacy Restrictions
Restrict settings for explicit content, purchases and downloads, and privacy.

Screen Time Passcode
Manage screen time for children from your own iPhone, or use a

Continue

Once Screen Time has been turned on, it can be turned off again by tapping once on the **Turn Off Screen Time** button at the bottom of the main Screen Time window in the Settings app, as shown in Step 6 on the next page.

4 Tap once on the **Continue** button

5 Screen Time can be set up for your own use, or on a child's iPhone. If it is set up for a child, there will be more parental control options for controlling the type of content that is available. Tap once on the required option

> **‹ Back**
>
> # Is This iPhone for Yourself or Your Child?
>
> Screen time for a child's iPhone lets you set up additional parental controls.
>
> **This is My iPhone**
>
> This is My Child's iPhone

6 The current Screen Time usage is shown at the top of the Screen Time settings screen. More Screen Time options are shown below – see pages 50-51

‹ Settings	**Screen Time**	
SCREEN TIME		Today at 13:14

Nick's iPhone >

13m

| Reading & Reference 6m | Entertainment 50s | Productivity 46s |

Downtime
Schedule time away from the screen. >

App Limits
Set time limits for apps. >

Always Allowed
Choose apps you want at all times. >

Content & Privacy Restrictions
Block inappropriate content. >

Use Screen Time Passcode

Use a passcode to secure Screen Time settings, and to allow for more time when limits expire.

Share Across Devices

You can enable this on any device signed in to iCloud to report your combined screen time.

Turn Off Screen Time

Hot tip

If Screen Time is set up for a child (**This is My Child's iPhone** option in Step 5), you can create a parental passcode that is required for a child to continue using the iPhone once one of the Screen Time restrictions has been reached. (See pages 52-53 for details.)

Don't forget

Each week the Screen Time option produces a report based on the overall usage, as shown in Step 6. The report is identified with a notification when it is published each week.

...cont'd

Options for Screen Time

Within the Screen Time settings there are options for viewing apps and content on your iPhone. Each of these is accessed on the main Screen Time settings page:

 Tap once on **Downtime**

 Drag the **Downtime** button to On and tap once on the **Start** and **End** buttons to select times for when only specified apps are available, then return to the Screen Time settings screen

 Tap once on **Always Allowed**

 The apps that are always allowed to operate, regardless of what settings there are for Screen Time, are displayed. Tap once on the red circle next to one to remove it. Tap once on a green circle to add an app to the Always Allowed apps, then return to the Screen Time settings screen

 Tap once on **Content & Privacy Restrictions**

 Drag the **Content & Privacy Restrictions** button to On to apply restrictions for blocking inappropriate content (see page 53 for details)

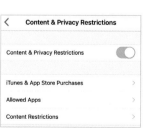

Don't forget

Content restrictions can be applied for content from the iTunes Store (such as age ratings for movies and TV shows), web content, and search content accessed by Siri, the iPhone's digital voice assistant.

7 Return to the Screen Time settings screen, then tap once on **App Limits**

> ⧗ **App Limits**
> Set time limits for apps.

8 Tap once on the **Add Limit** button to add time limits for using types of apps

> ‹ Screen Time   **App Limits**
>
> Set daily time limits for app categories you want to manage. App limits reset every day at midnight.
>
> Add Limit

9 Select a category for the types of apps that you want to limit use of (or select **All Apps & Categories**)

> Cancel   **Choose Apps**   Add
>
> CATEGORIES
>
> ✓ ≋   All Apps & Categories
>
> ○ 💬   Social Networking
>   WhatsApp, Messages, and 2 more
>
> ○ 🚀   Games
>
> ○ 🗑   Entertainment
>   Amazon Alexa, TV, and 4 more

10 Drag here to specify a time limit for using apps within the category selected in the previous step. By default, this is for each day. Tap once on the **Customize Days** button to set different time limits for specific days

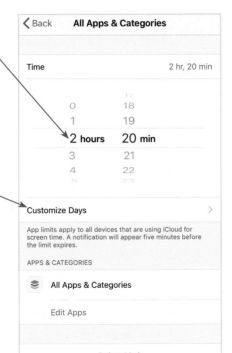

> ‹ Back   **All Apps & Categories**
>
> Time   2 hr, 20 min
>
> 0   18
> 1   19
> **2 hours   20 min**
> 3   21
> 4   22
>
> Customize Days   ›
>
> App limits apply to all devices that are using iCloud for screen time. A notification will appear five minutes before the limit expires.
>
> APPS & CATEGORIES
>
> ≋   All Apps & Categories
>
> Edit Apps
>
> Delete Limit

The time limit for using apps is only a suggestion, and the apps do not stop operating when the limit is reached. Instead, a notification appears to alert you to the fact that the time limit has been reached. Tap once on the **Ignore Limit** button to continue using the app.

> ⧗
> **Time Limit**
> You've reached your limit on Music.
> Ignore Limit

Select an option for how long you want to ignore the time limit.

> Remind Me in 15 Minutes
>
> Ignore Limit For Today
>
> Cancel

Enabling restrictions for children in Screen Time is a new feature in iOS 12.

Drag the **Block At End of Limit** button to On on the App Limits page that is accessed from Step 3, to ensure that apps cannot continue to be used after the time limit unless a parental passcode is entered.

Block At End of Limit	⬤

Restrictions for Children

If children or grandchildren have access to an iPhone, this can raise genuine concerns about the type of content that they may be accessing, and also the amount of time that they spend on the device. The Screen Time options can be used to apply specific settings for a child, so that you can have a degree of control over what they are using. These are similar to the standard Screen Time options, but they can be set up with an initial selection of wizards, and it is also possible to include a parental passcode that has to be entered when limits are reached. To set up restrictions for children:

1 Access Screen Time options as shown on page 48, and tap once on the **This is My Child's iPhone** button

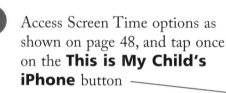

2 Select options for **Downtime**, for when the device cannot be used, by tapping on the **Start** and **End** options and specifying a time for each. Tap once on the **Set Downtime** button to apply these times

3 On the **App Limits** screen, tap once on the category of apps that you want to restrict and tap once on the **Set App Limit** button. Enter time controls as shown in Step 10 on page 51

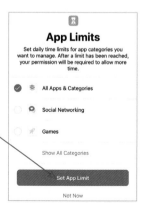

4 On the **Content & Privacy** screen, tap once on the **Continue** button

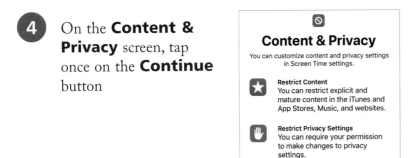

5 Create a parental passcode that will be required to access any restricted content, or override a time limit once it has been reached

A passcode can also be created for your own Screen Time settings. This prevents anyone else from changing these settings, and can be used to allow more time once a time limit is reached.

6 Tap once on the **Content & Privacy Restrictions** option, as shown on page 50. Drag the **Content & Privacy Restrictions** button to On to access the available options. These include options for limiting **iTunes & App Store Purchases**, specifying **Allowed Apps**, and selecting **Content Restrictions** for media such as movies, TV shows, music, and books that have been downloaded from the iTunes Store

If you are setting restrictions for a child or a grandchild, tell them about it and explain what you are doing and why.

About Apple Pay

Apple Pay is Apple's service for mobile, contactless payment. It can be used by adding credit, debit, and store cards to your iPhone via the Wallet app, and then paying for items by using your Face ID (or Touch ID for older iPhones) as authorization for payment. Credit, debit, and store cards have to be issued by banks or retailers who support Apple Pay, and there are an increasing number that do so, with more joining on a regular basis. Outlets also have to support Apple Pay but this, too, is increasing and, given the success of the iPhone, is likely to grow at a steady rate.

Setting up Apple Pay

To use Apple Pay you have to first add your cards to your iPhone (and be signed in to iCloud):

Don't forget

At the time of printing, Apple Pay has no limit for in-store purchases in the US and the UK.

Hot tip

Cards can also be added to the Wallet at any time from **Settings** > **Wallet & Apple Pay** > **Add Card**. This can also be used to create cash payments to people, using the Messages app. See page 103 for details.

Don't forget

If your bank does not yet support Apple Pay then you will not be able to add your credit or debit card details to the Wallet app.

1. Tap once on the **Wallet** app

2. Tap once on the **Add Credit or Debit Card** link, or tap once on this button

3. Tap once on the **Continue** button

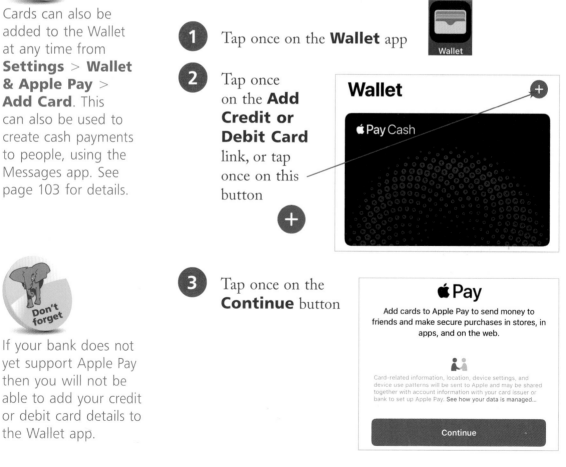

4 The card details can be added to the Wallet app by taking a photo of the card. Place the card on a flat surface, and position it within the white box. The card number is then added automatically. Alternatively, tap once on **Enter Card Details Manually**

< Back

Add Card

Position your card in the frame.

Enter Card Details Manually

Beware

Obtaining your card number using the camera is not always completely accurate. Take the photo in good light, always check the number afterwards, and amend it if necessary.

5 Once the card details have been added, your bank or store card issuer has to verify your card. This can be done either by a text message or a phone call

6 Once the Apple Pay wizard is completed, details of the card appear in the Wallet app

FROM SANTANDER

"Santander Debit Card" is ready for Apple Pay.

Don't forget

Although no form of contactless payment is 100% secure, Apple Pay does offer some security safeguards. One is that no card information is passed between the retailer and the user; the transaction is done by sending an encrypted token that is used to authorize the payment. Also, the use of the Face ID process ensures another step of authorization that is not available with all other forms of contactless payment.

7 To pay for items with Apple Pay, open the **Wallet** app and tap once on the card you want to use. Hold your iPhone up to the contactless payment card reader. Press the **On/Off** button twice and look at the phone screen to authorize the payment with Face ID. (Retailers must have a contactless card reader in order for Apple Pay to be used)

Face ID

55

Beware

There is no separate headphone jack on the iPhone. Instead, headphones are connected via the Lightning Connector jack. However, this means that earphones and headphones with a traditional jack will not work with the iPhone, unless the Lightning to 3.5mm headphone jack adapter is used (this is not included with the iPhone).

Don't forget

All models of the iPhone can be used with the AirPods; the wireless headphones from Apple.

Using the EarPods

The iPhone EarPods are not only an excellent way to listen to music and other audio on your iPhone; they can also be used in a variety of ways with the phone function:

The EarPods contain three main controls:

Down volume   Up volume

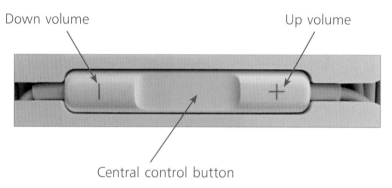

Central control button

- Plug in the EarPods to use them to hear someone who is calling you. Speak normally, and the other person will be able to hear you via the EarPods' in-built microphone.

- Click once in the middle of the control button to answer an incoming call.

- Press and hold in the middle of the control button for a couple of seconds (until you hear two beeps) to decline an incoming call.

- Click once in the middle of the control button to end the current call.

- If you are on a call and receive another one, click once on the middle of the control button to put the first call on hold and activate the second call.

- Press and hold the middle of the control button to dial a number using Voice Control, whereby you can speak the required number.

- Click on the control button when playing a music track to pause it. Click again to restart it. Double-click on the control button to move to the next track. Triple-click on the control button to move back to the previous track.

3 Head in the iCloud

iCloud, the online storage service, is at the heart of the iPhone for backing up your content and sharing it with other family members.

What is iCloud?

iCloud is the Apple online storage and backup service that performs a number of valuable functions:

- It makes your content available across multiple devices. The content is stored in the iCloud and then pushed out to other iCloud-enabled devices, including the iPad, iPod Touch, and other Mac or Windows computers.

- It enables online access to your content via the iCloud website. This includes your iCloud email, photos, contacts, calendar, reminders, and documents.

- It can back up the content on your iPhone.

To use iCloud you must have an Apple ID. This can be done when you first set up your iPhone, or at a later date. Once you have registered for and set up iCloud, it works automatically so you do not have to worry about anything.

It is free to register and set up a standard iCloud account.

An Apple ID can be created with an email address and password. It can then be used to access a variety of services, including the iTunes Store, Books, and the App Store.

To access your iCloud account through the website, access www.icloud.com and enter your Apple ID details.

① Tap once on the **Settings** app

② At the top of the Settings panel, tap once on the **Sign in to your iPhone** option

③ If you already have an Apple ID, enter your details and tap once on the **Sign In** button

④ If you do not yet have an Apple ID, tap once on the **Don't have an Apple ID or forgot it?** link and follow the steps to create your Apple ID

iCloud Settings

Once you have set up your iCloud account, you can then apply settings for how it works. Once you have done this, you will not have to worry about it again:

1. Tap once on the **Apple ID** section in the Settings app

2. Tap once on the **iCloud** button

3. Drag these buttons to **On** for each item that you wish to be included in iCloud. Each item is then saved and stored in the iCloud and made available to your other iCloud-enabled devices

Adding iCloud Storage

By default, you get 5GB of free storage space with an iCloud account. However, you can upgrade this if you want to increase the amount of storage. To do this:

If you have a lot of photos stored in iCloud then you may want to consider increasing your amount of storage.

Hot tip

Another useful iCloud function is the iCloud Keychain (**Settings** > **iCloud** > **Keychain**). If this is enabled, it can keep all of your passwords and credit card information up-to-date across multiple devices and remember them when you use them on websites. The information is encrypted and controlled through your Apple ID.

1 Access **iCloud** in Settings, as shown on page 59

2 Tap once on the **Manage Storage** button to view how your iCloud storage is being used

3 Tap once on the **Change Storage Plan** button if you want to change the amount of iCloud storage

4 Tap once on one of the storage options to buy this amount of iCloud storage. (Note: charges appear in your local currency.) Tap once on the amount of storage you require, to complete the change of storage

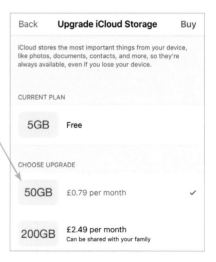

Backing up with iCloud

All of the items that you have assigned to iCloud
(see page 59) should be backed up there automatically.
However, if this is not happening you may need to turn on
the iCloud Backup. To do this:

1 Within the
iCloud section
of the Settings app,
tap once on the **iCloud Backup** button, if it is Off

2 The iCloud
Backup button
will be **Off**

3 Drag the **iCloud Backup** button to **On** to enable
automatic backup for iCloud. This has to be done
over Wi-Fi, with the iPhone locked and plugged in

4 You can also back up manually at any time by
tapping once on the **Back Up Now** button

Hot tip

You can also back
up your iPhone to
a computer that
has iTunes. Connect
the iPhone to the
computer with the
Lightning/USB cable,
and open iTunes.
Click on
this button
on the top
toolbar and, under
the **Summary** tab,
click on the **Back Up
Now** button under
the **Manually Back
up and Restore**
heading.

61

About Family Sharing

As everyone gets more and more digital devices it is becoming increasingly important to be able to share content with other people, particularly family members. In iOS 12, the Family Sharing function enables you to share items that you have downloaded from the App Store, such as music and movies, with up to six other family members, as long as they have an Apple ID Account. Once this has been set up, it is also possible to share items such as family calendars and photos, and even see where family members are on a map. To set up and start using Family Sharing:

Beware

To use Family Sharing, the other members of the group need to have iOS 8 (or later) installed on their mobile devices, or OS X Yosemite (or later) on an Apple desktop or laptop computer.

1 Access the Apple ID section within the Settings app, as shown on page 59

2 Tap once on the **Set Up Family Sharing...** link

> ☁ Set Up Family Sharing...

3 Tap once on the **Get Started** button

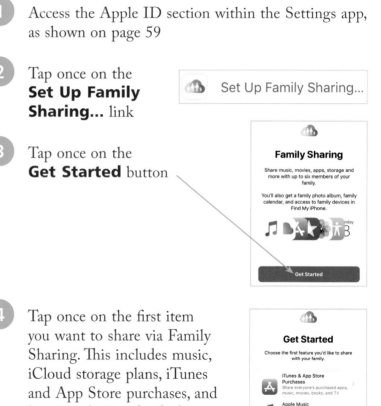

4 Tap once on the first item you want to share via Family Sharing. This includes music, iCloud storage plans, iTunes and App Store purchases, and location sharing for finding a lost or stolen Apple device

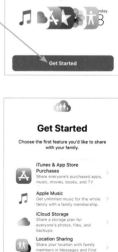

5 Tap once on the **Continue** button again to confirm your Apple ID account for Family Sharing

6 If you are the organizer of Family Sharing, payments will be taken from the credit/debit card that you registered when you set up your Apple ID. Tap once on the **Continue** button to confirm this

7 Once Family Sharing has been created, return to the iCloud section in the Settings app and tap once on the **Invite Via iMessage** button

8 Enter the name or email address of a family member, and tap once on the **Send** button

9 An invitation is sent to the selected person. They have to accept this before they can participate in Family Sharing

Hot tip

When you invite someone to Family Sharing you can specify that they have to ask permission before downloading content from the iTunes Store, the App Store, or the Books Store. To do this, select the family member in the **Family** section of the **iCloud** settings, and drag the **Ask To Buy** button to **On**. Each time they want to buy something you will be sent a notification asking for approval. This is a good option if grandchildren are added to the Family Sharing group.

Using Family Sharing

Once you have set up Family Sharing and added family members, you can start sharing a selection of items.

Sharing photos

Photos can be shared with Family Sharing, with the Family album that is created automatically within the Photos app.

Beware

Photo Sharing has to be turned **On** to enable Family Sharing for photos (**Settings** > **Photos** > **Shared Albums**).

Hot tip

When someone else in your Family Sharing circle adds a photo to the Family album, you are notified in the Notification Center and also by a red notification on the Photos app.

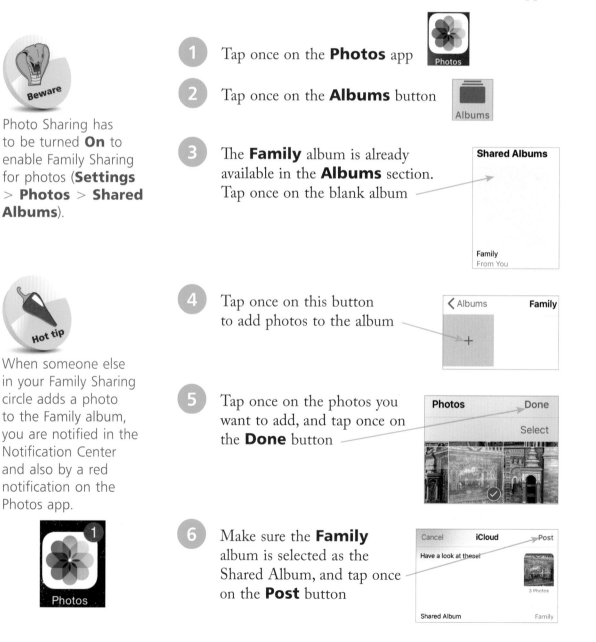

1 Tap once on the **Photos** app

2 Tap once on the **Albums** button

3 The **Family** album is already available in the **Albums** section. Tap once on the blank album

Shared Albums

Family
From You

4 Tap once on this button to add photos to the album

< Albums   Family

5 Tap once on the photos you want to add, and tap once on the **Done** button

Photos   Done
                Select

6 Make sure the **Family** album is selected as the Shared Album, and tap once on the **Post** button

Cancel   iCloud   Post
Have a look at these!

3 Photos

Shared Album   Family

Sharing calendars

Family Sharing also generates a Family calendar that can be used by all Family Sharing members:

1 Tap once on the **Calendar** app

2 Tap once on this button to create a New Event. The current calendar will probably not be the Family one. Tap once on the calendar name to change it

3 Tap once on the **Family** calendar

> **New Event   Calendar**
>
> ● Home   ✓
>
> ● Family

> Cancel   **New Event**   Add
>
> Fancy dress party
>
> Edinburgh   ⊗
>
> All-day   ○
>
> Starts   May 12, 2019   19:00
>
> Ends   23:00
>
> Repeat   Never >
>
> Travel Time   None >
>
> Calendar   ● Home >

4 The **Family** calendar is now selected for the event

> Calendar   ● Family >

5 Complete the details for the event. It will be added to your calendar, with the **Family** tag. Other people in your Family Sharing circle will have this event added to their Family calendar too, and they will be sent a notification

> 19:00
> **Fancy dress party**
> Edinburgh
> 20:00
> 21:00
> 22:00
> 23:00
> 00:00
>
> Today   Calendars   Inbox (3)

Don't forget

When someone in the Family Sharing circle adds an event to the Family calendar it will appear in your calendar with the appropriate tag. A red notification will also appear on the Calendar app, and it will appear in the Notification Center (if the Calendar has been selected to appear here).

Don't forget

Tap once on the **Add** button to invite other people by email (they do not have to be part of Family Sharing, but they do have to accept your invitation to be part of Find My Friends).

Don't forget

Tap once on your own name at the bottom-left of the screen to see your settings for Find My Friends. This is where you can share your location. Share My Location also has to be turned on within **Settings** > **Privacy** > **Location Services** > **Share My Location**.

Me
Great Britain

...cont'd

Finding family members

Family Sharing makes it easy to keep in touch with the rest of the family and see exactly where they are. This can be done with the Find Friends app. The other person must have their iPhone (or other Apple device) turned on, be online and be sharing their location. To do this:

1 Tap once on the **Find Friends** app

2 Your own location has to be shared if you want other people to see it. Tap once on the **Me** button at the bottom of the window, and drag the **Share My Location** button to On

3 The details of any people who are linked via your Family Sharing are displayed. Tap once on a person's name to view their details and location in the top panel (if they are online and have shared their location on their device)

Sharing apps, music, books and movies

Family Sharing means that all members of the group can share purchases from the iTunes Store, the App Store, or the Books store. To do this:

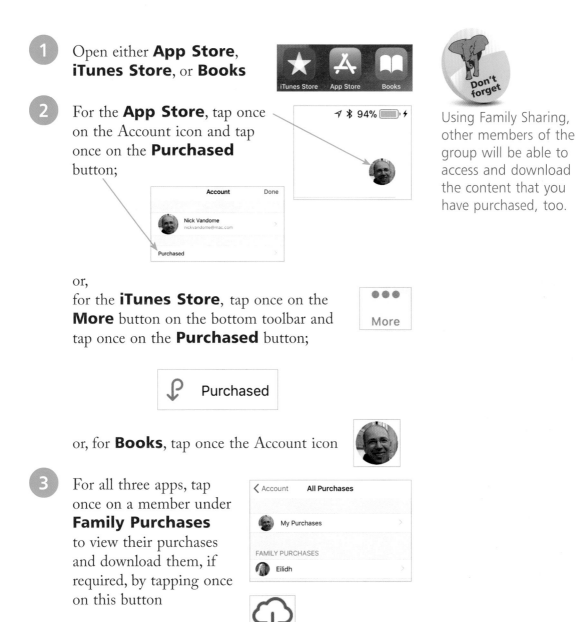

1 Open either **App Store**, **iTunes Store**, or **Books**

2 For the **App Store**, tap once on the Account icon and tap once on the **Purchased** button;

or,

for the **iTunes Store**, tap once on the **More** button on the bottom toolbar and tap once on the **Purchased** button;

or, for **Books**, tap once the Account icon

3 For all three apps, tap once on a member under **Family Purchases** to view their purchases and download them, if required, by tapping once on this button

Using Family Sharing, other members of the group will be able to access and download the content that you have purchased, too.

iCloud Drive and the Files App

One of the features of iCloud is the iCloud Drive, which can be used to store documents such as those created with the Apple suite of productivity apps (available in the App Store): Pages (word processing), Numbers (spreadsheets), and Keynote (presentations). These documents can then be accessed with the Files app.

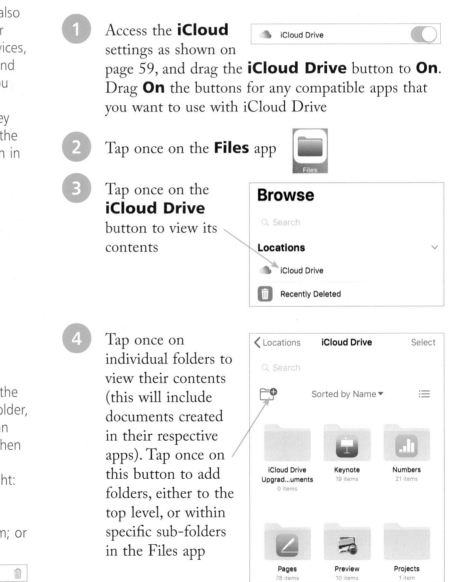

Hot tip

The Files app can also be used with other online storage services, such as Dropbox and Google Drive, if you have one of these accounts. If so, they will appear under the **Locations** section in Step 3.

Hot tip

Tap once on the **Select** button at the top of any open folder, and tap once on an item to select it. Then use these buttons to, from left to right: share the selected item; duplicate an item; move an item; or delete an item.

1 Access the **iCloud** settings as shown on page 59, and drag the **iCloud Drive** button to **On**. Drag **On** the buttons for any compatible apps that you want to use with iCloud Drive

2 Tap once on the **Files** app

3 Tap once on the **iCloud Drive** button to view its contents

4 Tap once on individual folders to view their contents (this will include documents created in their respective apps). Tap once on this button to add folders, either to the top level, or within specific sub-folders in the Files app

4 Calls and Contacts

One of the main uses for the iPhone is still to make and receive phone calls. This chapter shows what you need for this.

Adding Contacts

Because of its power and versatility, it is sometimes forgotten that one of the reasons for the iPhone's existence is to make phone calls. Before you start doing this, it is a good idea to add family and friends to the Contacts app. This will enable you to phone them without having to tap in their phone number each time. To add a contact:

1 Tap once on the **Contacts** app

2 Any contacts that you already have are displayed

3 Tap once on this button to add a new contact

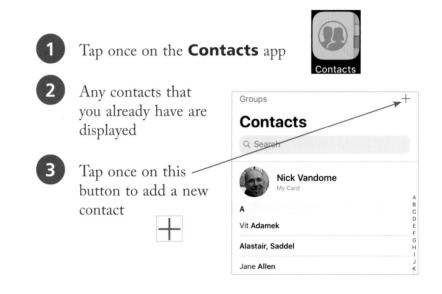

4 Enter the name for the contact at the top of the window, in the **First name** and **Last name** fields

Don't forget

Tap once on the green button next to a field to add another field. Tap once on a red button to delete a field.

5 Tap once in one of the Phone fields, or tap once on the **add phone** button to add a new Phone field

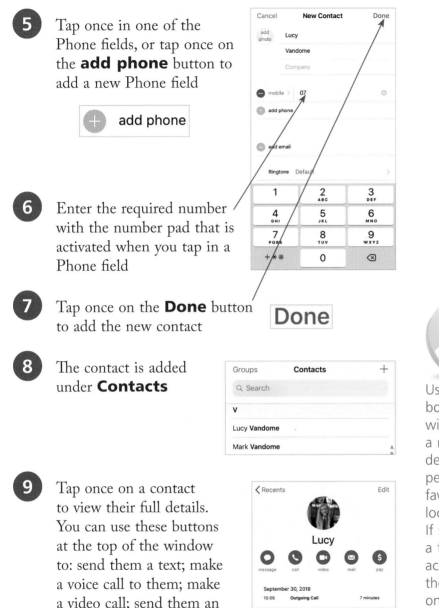

6 Enter the required number with the number pad that is activated when you tap in a Phone field

7 Tap once on the **Done** button to add the new contact

Done

8 The contact is added under **Contacts**

9 Tap once on a contact to view their full details. You can use these buttons at the top of the window to: send them a text; make a voice call to them; make a video call; send them an email (if their email address is included); or send them money via Apple Pay (if this is available)

Hot tip

Use the buttons at the bottom of a contact's window to send them a message, share their details with other people, add them as a favorite or share your location with them. If someone is added as a favorite, they can be accessed directly from the **Favorites** button on the bottom toolbar of the **Phone** app.

71

Making a Call

The iPhone can be used to make calls to specific phone numbers that you enter manually, or to contacts in your Contacts app.

Dialing a number

To make a call by dialing a specific number, first tap once on the **Phone** app.

You must have a SIM card inserted in your iPhone and an appropriate cellular/ mobile service provider in order to make a call with the **Phone** app, unless it is through an app that uses Wi-Fi, such as FaceTime – see pages 118-119.

1 Tap once on the **Keypad** button at the bottom of the window

Keypad

Tap once on the **Voicemail** button on the bottom toolbar to view any messages here. If you have any, there will be a red notification icon on the Voicemail button.

2 Tap on the numbers on the keypad to enter the number, which appears at the top of the window. Tap on this button to delete a number that has been entered

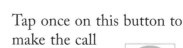

3 Tap once on this button to make the call

Calling a contact

To call someone who has been added to the Contacts app:

1 Open the **Phone** app, and tap once on the **Contacts** button at the bottom of the window. The Contacts app opens, with the Phone toolbar still visible at the bottom of the window

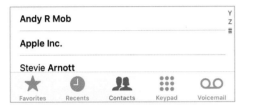

2 Tap once on a contact

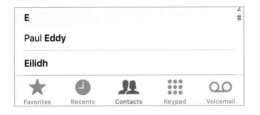

3 The full details for the contact are displayed. Tap once on the **call** button at the top of the window to call the number of the contact

To find someone in the Contacts app (either directly from the app, or from the **Contacts** button in the Phone app), swipe up and down on the screen; enter a name in the Search box at the top of the window; or tap on a letter on the alphabetic list down the right-hand side.

73

Receiving a Call

When you receive a call, there are four main options:

Don't forget

When a call is connected, the following buttons appear on the screen. Use them to: mute a call; access the keypad again, in case you need to add any more information such as for an automated call; access the speaker so you do not have to keep the phone at your ear; add another call to create a conference call; make a FaceTime call to the caller (if they have this facility); or access your Contacts app.

1 When you receive a call, the person's name and photo (if they have been added to your Contacts) or number appears at the top of the screen

2 Tap once on the **Accept** button (or if the phone is locked, drag the **slide to answer** button to the right) to take the call

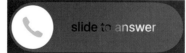

3 Tap once on the **Decline** button to decline the call, without any other actions. If the phone is locked when a call comes in, press the phone's **On/Off** button to decline the call. This is then displayed at the top of the window

4 Tap once on the **Remind Me** button to decline the call but set a reminder for yourself that the person has called

5 Select an option for when you want to be reminded

The reminder in Step 5 will appear on the Lock screen and also as a notification in the Notification Center (if this has been specified).

6 Tap once on the **Message** button to decline the call but send the person a text message instead

7 Tap once on the text message that you want to send

Tap once on this button to end a call.

Saving Phone Contacts

Another quick way to add a contact is to ask someone to phone you so that you can then copy their number directly from your phone to your Contacts. You do not even have to answer the phone to do this.

1 Once someone has phoned, tap once on the **Phone** app

2 Tap once on the **Recents** button at the bottom of the window

3 The call will be displayed. Tap once on the **i** symbol

Recents

| All | Missed | Edit |

08
unknown   Thursday

4 Information about the call is displayed, including the number

5 Tap once on the **Create New Contact** button

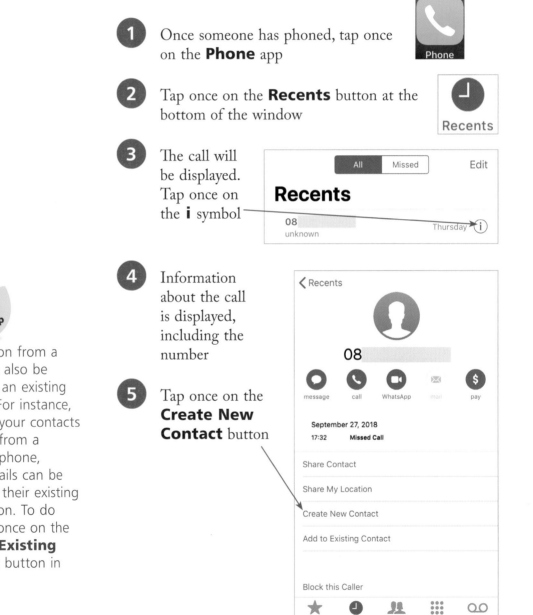

‹ Recents

08

message   call   WhatsApp   mail   pay

September 27, 2018
17:32   Missed Call

Share Contact

Share My Location

Create New Contact

Add to Existing Contact

Block this Caller

Favorites   Recents   Contacts   Keypad   Voicemail

Hot tip

Information from a caller can also be added to an existing contact. For instance, if one of your contacts calls you from a different phone, these details can be added to their existing information. To do this, tap once on the **Add to Existing Contact** button in Step 5.

The **New Contact** window opens, with the number already pre-inserted

Cancel	**New Contact**	Done

add photo

First name

Last name

Company

— phone > 08

+ add phone

 Add information for the contact as required, such as name, any additional phone numbers, and email

Cancel	**New Contact**	Done

add photo

Martin

Williams ⊗

Company

— phone > 08

+ add phone

 Tap once on the **Done** button to add the new contact

Setting Ringtones

Ringtones were one of the original "killer apps" for mobile/cell phones: the must-have accessory that helped transform the way people looked at these devices. The iPhone has a range of ringtones that can be used, and you can also download and install thousands more. To use the default ringtones:

Tap once on the **Tone Store** button in the Ringtone window to go to the iTunes Store, where you can download more ringtones, from the **Tones** button.

Tone Store

78

If the Ringer button on the side of the iPhone is turned Off, the iPhone can still be set to vibrate if a call or notification is received, using the **Vibrate on Silent** button at the top of the main Sounds & Haptics window (drag the button to **On**).

1 Tap once on the **Settings** app

2 Tap once on the **Sounds & Haptics** tab

Sounds & Haptics

3 Tap once on the **Ringtone** link under **Sounds and Vibration Patterns** to select ringtones for when you receive a phone call

SOUNDS AND VIBRATION PATTERNS
Ringtone — Reflection >

4 Tap once on one of the options to hear a preview and select it

RINGTONES
Reflection (Default)
Apex
Beacon
✓ Bulletin

5 Sounds and vibrations can also be selected for a range of other items such as text messages, email, and calendar and reminder alerts, by going back to the Sounds and Vibration Patterns section and choosing a tone for each item

SOUNDS AND VIBRATION PATTERNS
Ringtone — Bulletin >
Text Tone — Vibrate Only >
New Voicemail — Tri-tone >
New Mail — Bamboo >
Sent Mail — Swoosh >
Calendar Alerts — Chord >
Reminder Alerts — Chord >

Adding individual ringtones

It is also possible to set ringtones for individual people, so that you know immediately who a call is from.

1 Select a contact in the Contacts app, and tap on the **Edit** button

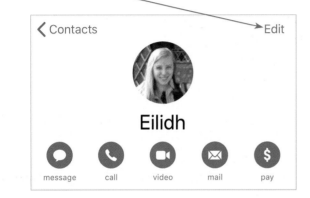

2 Tap once on the **Ringtone** button

3 Tap once on a ringtone to assign this to the contact

Only set ringtones for your most regular contacts, otherwise you may end up with too many variations.

If you are going to be using your iPhone around other people, consider turning the **Keyboard Clicks** option (at the bottom of the main **Sounds & Haptics** Settings window) to **Off**, as the noise can get annoying for those in the vicinity.

Phone Settings

As with most of the iPhone functions, there is a range of settings for the phone itself. To use them:

1 Tap once on the **Settings** app

2 Tap once on the **Phone** tab

80

3 The Phone settings have options for responding with a text to a call that you do not take; call forwarding; call waiting; and blocking unwanted callers

4 Tap once on the **Respond with Text** button to create a text message that can be sent if you do not want to answer a call when it is received

5 Typing and Texts

This chapter shows how to get used to the virtual keyboard for adding text, and how to use the texting options, including the range of items that can be added to messages with iOS 12, which include animated animoji and memoji stickers.

The iPhone Keyboard

The keyboard on the iPhone is a virtual one; i.e. it appears on the touchscreen whenever text or numbered input is required for an app. This can be for a variety of reasons:

- Entering text with a word processing app, or into an email or an organizing app such as Notes.

- Entering a web address in a web browser such as the Safari app.

- Entering information into an online form.

- Entering a password.

Viewing the keyboard

When you attempt one of the actions above, the keyboard appears so that you can enter any text or numbers:

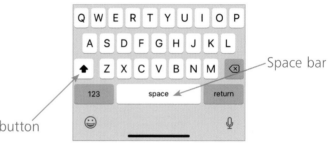

Space bar

Shift button

Around the keyboard

To access the various keyboard controls:

Hot tip

In some apps such as Notes, Mail and Messages, it is possible to change the keyboard into a trackpad for moving the cursor. To do this, press and hold firmly on the keyboard, and then swipe over the trackpad to move the cursor around.

Hot tip

It is possible to increase the size of the iPhone keyboard with the **Zoom** feature within the Accessibility settings. See pages 182-183 for details.

Don't forget

To return from Caps Lock, tap once on the **Caps** button.

1. Tap once on the **Shift** button to create a **Cap** (capital) text letter

2. Double-tap on the **Shift** button to enable **Caps Lock**

3. Tap once on this button to back-delete an item

4 Tap once on this button to access the **Numbers** keyboard option

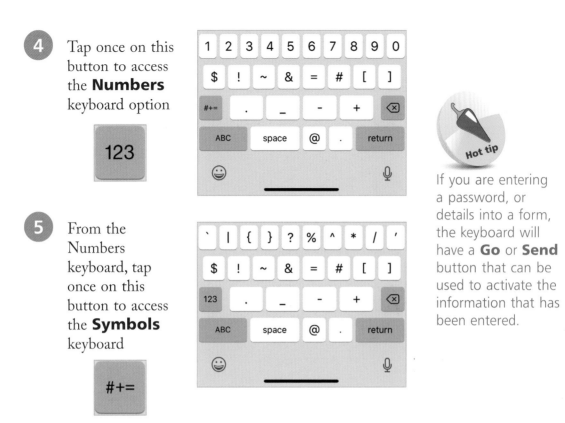

5 From the Numbers keyboard, tap once on this button to access the **Symbols** keyboard

If you are entering a password, or details into a form, the keyboard will have a **Go** or **Send** button that can be used to activate the information that has been entered.

6 Tap once on this button on either of the two keyboards above to return to the standard QWERTY option

ABC

Shortcut keys

Instead of having to go to a different keyboard every time you want to add punctuation (or numbers), there is a shortcut for this:

1 Press and hold on the **Numbers** button, and swipe over the item you want to include. This will be added, and you will remain on the QWERTY keyboard

Several keys have additional options that can be accessed by pressing and holding on the key. A lot of these are letters that have accented versions in different languages; e.g. a, e, i, o and u. Swipe across a letter to add it.

Keyboard Settings

Settings for the keyboard can be determined in the General section of the Settings app. To do this:

Hot tip

Drag the **Predictive** button to **On** to enable predictive texting (see pages 86-87). Drag the **Character Preview** button to **On** to show a magnified example of a letter or symbol when it is pressed, to ensure that the correct one is selected.

Hot tip

The Auto-Correction function works as you type a word, so it may change a number of times, depending on the length of the word you are typing.

1 Tap once on the **Settings** app

2 Tap once on the **General** tab

3 Tap once on the **Keyboard** link

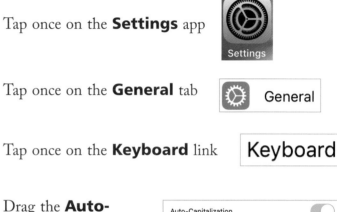

4 Drag the **Auto-Capitalization** button to **On** to automatically capitalize letters at the beginning of a sentence

5 Drag the **Auto-Correction** button to **On** to enable suggestions for words to appear as you type, particularly if you have mistyped a word

6 Drag the **Check Spelling** and **Smart Punctuation** buttons to **On** to identify misspelled words (with red underlining) and add punctuation

7 Drag the **Enable Caps Lock** button to **On** to enable this function to be performed

8 Drag the **"." Shortcut** button to **On** to add a period (full stop) and a space to start a new sentence by just tapping the space bar twice

9 Tap once on the **Text Replacement** link to view existing text shortcuts and also to create new ones

> **General**   **Keyboards**
>
> Keyboards   2 >
>
> Text Replacement   >

10 Tap once on this button to create new shortcuts

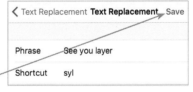

> **< Keyboards** **Text Replacement**   **+**
>
> Q Search
>
> **A**
> ah   At home
> **M**
> mnn   My name is Nick
> **O**
> omw   On my way

Hot tip

With iOS 12, third-party keyboards can be downloaded from the App Store and used instead of the default one. One to look at is SwiftKey Keyboard.

11 Enter a phrase and the shortcut you want to use to create it when you type. Tap once on the **Save** button

> **< Text Replacement** **Text Replacement** Save
>
> Phrase   See you layer
>
> Shortcut   syl

12 Tap once on the **Keyboards** button in Step 9 to add a new keyboard

13 Tap once on the **Add New Keyboard...** button

> Add New Keyboard...

14 Tap once on a keyboard to add it. The keyboard will be available by selecting the globe icon (see the Don't Forget tip)

> Cancel   **Add New Keyboard**
>
> SUGGESTED KEYBOARDS
>
> English (United States)
>
> OTHER IPHONE KEYBOARDS
>
> English (Australia)
>
> English (Canada)
>
> English (India)

Don't forget

By default, two keyboards are installed: one for the language of your region, and the emoji one. If more keyboards are added, this symbol will appear on the keyboard. Press on it to select another keyboard from the one being used. If only the two default keyboards are installed, this symbol will be the emoji one.

Using Predictive Text

Predictive text tries to guess what you are typing, and also predicts the next word following the one you have just typed. It is excellent for text messaging.

To use it:

 Tap once on the **General** tab in the Settings app

 General

 Tap once on the **Keyboard** link

Keyboard >

 Drag the **Predictive** button **On**

Predictive

 When predictive text is activated, the QuickType bar is displayed above the keyboard. Initially, this has a suggestion for the first word to include. Tap on a word, or start typing

Don't forget

Predictive text learns from your writing style as you write, and so gets more accurate at predicting words. It can also recognize a change in style for different apps such as Mail and Messages.

 As you type, suggestions appear. Tap on one to accept it. Tap on the word within the quotation marks to accept exactly what you have typed

6 If you continue typing, the predictive suggestions will change as you add more letters

7 After you have typed a word, a suggestion for the next word appears. Tap on one of the suggestions or start typing a new word, which will then also have predictive suggestions as you type

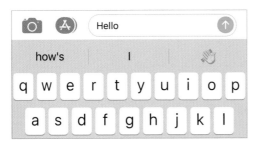

Toggling predictive text from the keyboard
You can also toggle predictive text On or Off from the keyboard. To do this:

1 Press and hold on this button on the keyboard

2 Tap once on the **Keyboard Settings...** button to access the **Predictive** setting, from where it can be turned **On** or **Off**

Hot tip

Tapping the button in Step 1 allows you to add Emojis, which are symbols used in text messages to signify happiness, surprise, sadness, etc. (See page 96 for details.)

One Handed Keyboard

When typing with the iPhone, this is frequently done with one hand. To make this easier, there is an option for formatting the keyboard for one handed typing. To do this:

 Open the **General** tab in the Settings app, and tap once on the **One Handed Keyboard** link

‹ General	Keyboards	
Keyboards		2 ›
Text Replacement		›
One Handed Keyboard		Off ›

 Select the **Left** or **Right** option for the keyboard

‹ Back	One Handed Keyboard
Off	
Left	✓
Right	

3 If more than one keyboard has been added (e.g. the emoji keyboard), press and hold on this button on the keyboard, and tap once on the options for moving the keyboard to the left or right

Keyboard Settings...

English (US)

Emoji

4 The keyboard is moved into the position selected in either Steps 2 or 3. Tap once here to revert to the original keyboard

Entering Text

Once you have applied the keyboard settings that you require, you can start entering text. To do this:

1 Tap once on the screen to activate the keyboard from the app. Start typing with the keyboard. The text will appear at the point where you tapped on the screen

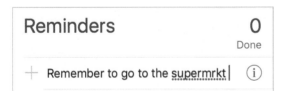

2 As you type, Auto-Correction comes up with suggestions (if it is turned on). Tap once on the space bar to accept the suggestion, or tap once on the cross next to it to reject it

3 If Check Spelling is enabled in the keyboard settings, any misspelled words appear underlined in red

4 Double-tap the space bar to enter a period (full-stop) and a space at the end of a sentence

If you keep typing as normal, the Auto-Correction suggestion will disappear when you finish the word.

If Predictive text is turned **On** (**Settings > General > Keyboard > Predictive**), the Auto-Correction suggestions will appear on the QuickType bar above the keyboard.

The **"."** **Shortcut** option has to be turned **On** (**Settings > General > Keyboard > "." Shortcut**) for the functionality in Step 4 to work (see page 84).

Editing Text

Once text has been entered it can be selected, copied, cut, and pasted. Depending on the app being used, the text can also be formatted, such as with a word processing app.

Selecting text

To select text and perform tasks on it:

Hot tip

Once the selection buttons have been accessed, tap once on **Select** to select the previous word, or **Select All** to select all of the text.

Hot tip

In some apps such as Notes, Mail, and Messages, it is possible to change the keyboard into a trackpad for moving the cursor. To do this, press and hold firmly on the keyboard, and then swipe over the trackpad to move the cursor around.

1 To change the insertion point, tap and hold until the magnifying glass appears

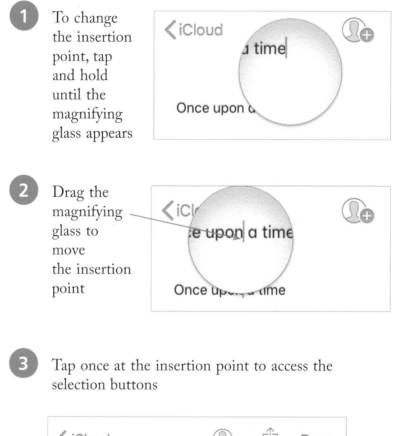

2 Drag the magnifying glass to move the insertion point

3 Tap once at the insertion point to access the selection buttons

4 Double-tap on a word to select it. Tap once on **Cut** or **Copy**, as required

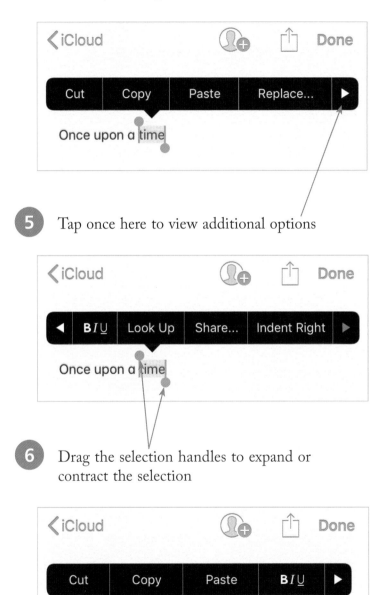

5 Tap once here to view additional options

6 Drag the selection handles to expand or contract the selection

Hot tip

The selection buttons in Steps 4 and 5 can also be used to replace the selected word; add bold, italics or underlining to it; view a definition (Look Up) of it; share it; or indent it. (These options may change depending on the app you're in, and whether the iPhone is held in portrait or landscape mode.)

Types of Text Messages

Text messaging should not be thought of as the domain of the younger generation. On your iPhone you can join the world of text with the Apple iMessage service that is accessed via the Messages app. This enables text, photo, video, and audio messages to be sent, free of charge, between users of iOS on the iPhone, iPad, iPod Touch, and Mac computers with OS X or macOS.

However, there are two different types of text messages:

- iMessages that are sent over Wi-Fi to other users with an Apple ID and using an iPhone, iPad, iPod Touch, or a Mac computer.

- Text messages that are just sent via your cellular (mobile) carrier.

Wi-Fi texts (iMessages)
When texts are sent over Wi-Fi, this can only be done with other users who have an Apple ID.

When you are connected to Wi-Fi, this symbol appears at the top of your iPhone.

To use iMessages over Wi-Fi, the **iMessage** button has to be **On** in the **Messages** section of the Settings app.

‹ Settings	**Messages**	
iMessage		◯

iMessages can be sent between iPhone, iPad, iPod touch, and Mac. Sending or receiving iMessages uses wireless data. Learn More...

Cellular (mobile) carrier texts (SMS)
When texts are sent via your mobile carrier, this can be done to any cellular (mobile) number.

When you are connected to your cellular (mobile) carrier, this symbol appears at the top of your iPhone, with the appropriate carrier's name.

Don't forget

In the **Messages** settings there is also an option to send texts as SMS when iMessages is unavailable. However, since this will then be sent using your cellular network, a charge may apply for the text.

Sending an iMessage via Wi-Fi

When you send an iMessage, it appears in a blue bubble.

If you enter a number that is not connected to an Apple ID account then the message will be sent as an SMS (green bubble) rather than an iMessage (blue bubble).

Sending a text via your carrier

When you send a text via your cellular (mobile) carrier, it appears in a green bubble.

iMessages can also be used to send money to other people. This is done using Apple Pay, and the recipient also has to have Apple Pay, enabled. See page 103 for details.

Text Messaging

The process for sending text messages is the same for either iMessages or SMS text messages:

1 Tap once on the **Messages** app

2 You have to sign in with your Apple ID before you can use Messages. Enter these details, and tap on the **Sign In** button

3 Tap once on this button to create a new message and start a new conversation

4 Tap once on this button to select someone from your contacts

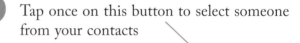

| New iMessage | Cancel |
| To: Eilidh, | ⊕ |

5 Tap once on a contact to select them as the recipient of the new message

| Groups | **Contacts** | Cancel |

Q Search

A

Vit **Adamek**

Alastair, Saddel

Jane **Allen**

Katriona **Allen**

A
B
C
D
E
F
G

Don't forget

You can also enter a cell/mobile phone number into the **To:** field for text messages in Messages. If this is connected to an Apple ID, the message will be sent as an iMessage; if not, it will be sent as an SMS message.

94

Hot tip

You can also add someone from your contacts by typing their name into the **To:** field shown in Step 4. As you start typing, names will appear for you to select from. You can type the telephone number of anyone who isn't in your contacts here, too.

...cont'd

6 Tap once here, and type with the keyboard to create a message

When a message has been sent, you are notified underneath it when it has been delivered.

95

7 Tap once on this button to send a message (it is not available until a message has been composed)

Press and hold on a message, and tap on the **More...** button that appears. Select a message, or messages, and tap on the **Trash** icon to remove them from the threads. (See pages 105-106 for more information on deleting messages.)

8 As the conversation progresses, each message is displayed in the main window

Enhancing Text Messages

Adding emojis

Emojis (small graphical symbols) are very popular in text messages, and there is now a huge range that can be included with iOS 12. To add these:

 1 Tap once on this button on the keyboard to view the emoji keyboards

 2 Swipe left and right to view the emoji options. Tap once on an emoji to add it to a message

Emojis can be added automatically from certain words:

 1 Add text, and tap once on the button in Step 1 above. The items that can be replaced are highlighted

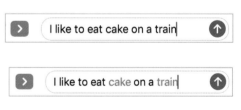

 2 Tap once on a highlighted word to see the emoji options. Tap once on one to add it to the message

Adding animojis

Introduced on the iPhone X with iOS 11, the animoji feature is now available on all new models of iPhone. Animojis are animated stickers that can take on the expressions and voice of the person looking at the iPhone's camera:

Beware

1 Create a new message or open an existing conversation

2 Tap once on the **Animoji** icon in the App Strip below the text box

Recipients of animojis should have an iPhone X or later, in order to view it accurately.

3 Swipe left and right to select the animoji icon, as required

4 Tap once on the **Record** button
to record facial expression for the animoji

5 Tap once on this button to finish recording

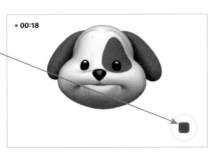

• 00:18

Don't forget

The expressions for an animoji can be recorded for up to 30 seconds.

6 Tap once on the **Send** button to send the animoji to the recipient of the message

...cont'd

Adding memojis

An extension of the animoji feature is the ability to create memojis in iOS 12 on the iPhone XR, XS and XS Max. These are customized avatars that can be created to look like yourself. To do this:

Adding memojis is a new feature in iOS 12.

1 Create a new message or open an existing conversation

2 Tap once on the **Animoji** icon in the App Strip below the text box

3 Swipe to the right and tap once on the **New Memoji** button

New Memoji

Hot tip

For each of the customizable options in Step 4, several different variations can be selected. For instance: for the Skin option, Color and Freckles can be selected; for the Head Shape option, Age and Chin can be selected; and for Facial Hair, there are options for selecting Sideburns and Mustache & Beard color and style.

4 The memoji starts as a blank avatar that can be customized. Swipe along the top bar to select options for **Skin**, **Hairstyle**, **Head Shape**, **Eyes**, **Brows**, **Nose & Lips**, **Ears**, **Facial Hair**, **Eyewear**, and **Headwear**

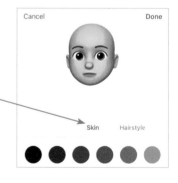

5 Tap once on the **Done** button to complete the memoji. It is added to the App Strip and can be added to a message by tapping on it here

Full-screen messages

iMessages can also be sent with full-screen effects:

Hot tip

1 Write a message, and press and hold on this button

2 Tap once on the **Screen** button at the top of the window

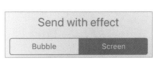

Screen

3 Different animated options can be selected to accompany the message

4 Swipe to the left, or tap on these buttons to view different animated effects

5 Tap once on this button to send the message (tap once on the cross to delete the animated effect)

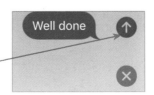

With Messages you can show people your location (by sending a map) rather than just telling them. To do this: once a conversation has started, tap once on the person's name at the top of the message window and tap once on the **info** button.

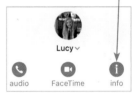

Tap once on **Send My Current Location**, or **Share My Location**.

Send My Current Location
Share My Location

If you select **Share My Location**, this will be updated if your location changes (as long as Location Services is turned On in **Settings** > **Privacy** > **Location Services**).

Hot tip

By default, the App Strip button is displayed at the left-hand side of the text box. However, as you start writing a message, this is replaced by the right-pointing arrow in Step 1. Tap once on this to access the App Strip button.

Hot tip

The other Bubble effects in Step 2 are **Slam**, **Loud** and **Gentle**. These determine how the speech bubble appears to the recipient: Slam moves in quickly from left to right; Loud appears initially as a large bubble; Gentle appears initially with small text in the speech bubble. After the initial effects, the bubble returns to its normal size.

...cont'd

Invisible messages

There are several ways to enhance text messages, including sending them in a digital version of invisible ink:

1. Write a message and press on this button

2. Tap once on the **Bubble** button at the top of the window

3. Tap once on the **Invisible Ink** button

4. Tap once on this button to send the invisible message

5. The message is sent as a bubble where the content is obscured

6. Swipe on the message to view its content

Handwritten messages

To create a more informal message, handwriting can be used.

1 Turn the iPhone into landscape mode, and tap once on this button on the keyboard to access the handwriting panel

2 Write using your finger, or select one of the pre-formatted messages at the bottom of the  panel. Tap once on the **Done** button to add it to a message. The text appears animated to the recipient, as if it is being written on their screen

Quick replies (Tapback)

Instead of writing a full reply to a message it is possible to add a quick reply (also known as Tapback), which consists of an appropriate icon that is attached to the original message:

1 Press and hold on the message to which you want to add a quick reply, and tap once on one of the icons

2 The selected icon is added to the original message, and this is displayed to the sender of the message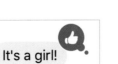

Hot tip

You can also send family and friends audio clips in an iMessage so that they can hear from you too. To do this, press and hold on the microphone icon at the right-hand side of the text box, and record your message.

101

...cont'd

Adding and stickers from the App Strip

Stickers and graphics are another option for enhancing text messages. To do this:

The App Strip has been redesigned in iOS 12 on the iPhone.

Tap once on this button in the App Strip to add photos or videos to a message. This is an enhanced feature in iOS 12.

Music from your iTunes Library and Digital Touch effects can be added to iMessages by tapping once on each of these buttons on the App Strip in Step 1. (Swipe to right to view them if they are not visible.)

1 Tap once on this button to the left of the text field box to access the App Strip

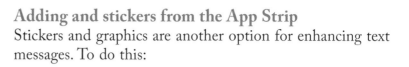

2 Tap once on this button on the bottom toolbar to access the App Store

3 Tap on the Search icon to search for items that can be added to messages, such as stickers

4 Navigate the content in the App Store to find apps to download as required; e.g. a set of stickers

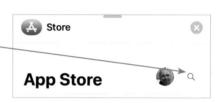

5 Downloaded items are available in the App Strip. Tap once on one to view its available content and add it

to a message by dragging it into the text box

Sending Money with Messages

Using Apple Pay, it is possible to send money to people using the Messages app. To do this:

1 Access **Settings > Wallet & Apple Pay** and tap once on the **Apple Pay Cash** button

Apple Pay Cash was introduced with iOS 11.2, but should become available in a wider range of locations with iOS 12. At the time of printing, Apple Pay Cash is only available in the US, but is expected to be rolled out in the UK and other regions.

2 Tap once on the **Continue** button to set up Apple Pay Cash, which can be used with the Messages app

3 To meet financial regulations, you have to verify your identity before using Apple Pay Cash. Tap once on the **Continue** button and enter your name and address to verify your identity to set up Apple Pay Cash

Verify Your Identity

Verify your personal information to continue sending and receiving money with Apple Pay.

The information you provide is used for fraud prevention and to comply with U.S. financial regulations. The information must match public records to allow us to verify your identity.

Don't forget

Payments are made from Apple Pay Cash, which is funded by the card, or cards, that have been added to Apple Pay. See pages 54-55 for details about adding cards.

4 Once Apple Pay Cash has been set up, payments can be made in the Messages app by opening an existing message, or starting a new one, and tapping once on the **Pay** button on the App Strip. Enter the amount to pay and tap once on the **Pay** button to send the payment

Beware

Recipients of payments must have Apple Pay and Apple Pay Cash set up on their iOS 12 device too.

Voice Typing

On the keyboard there is also a voice typing option, which enables you to enter text by speaking into a microphone, rather than typing on the keyboard. This is On by default.

Using voice typing

Voice typing (dictation) can be used with any app with a text input function. To do this:

Voice typing is not an exact science, and you may find that some strange examples appear. The best results are created if you speak as clearly as possible and reasonably slowly.

Dictation can be turned **On** or **Off** in **Settings** > **General** > **Keyboard** > **Enable Dictation**.

There are other voice typing apps available from the App Store. One to try is Dragon Anywhere.

1. Tap once on this button on the keyboard to activate the voice typing microphone. Speak into the microphone to record text

2. As the voice typing function is processing the recording, this screen appears

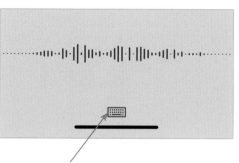

3. Tap once on the **Keyboard** button to finish recording and return to the standard keyboard

4. Once the recording has been processed, the text appears in the app

Managing Messages

Text conversations with individuals can become quite lengthy so it is sometimes a good idea to remove some messages, while still keeping the conversation going.

1 As a conversation with one person progresses, it moves downwards in the window

Hot tip

You can copy a message by tapping once on the **Copy** button in Step 2 and then pasting it into another app, such as an email. To do this, press and hold on an open email, and tap once on the **Paste** button.

2 Press and hold on a message that you want to delete, and tap once on the **More...** button (pressing and holding on a message also activates the Tapback option; see page 101)

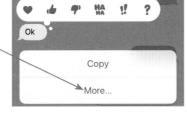

3 Tap once next to any message that you want to delete, so that a white tick in a blue circle appears

Hot tip

Settings for the Messages app can be applied in the Settings app. These include: Send Read Receipts, to indicate that you have read the message sent; and to send SMS messages when iMessage is unavailable.

4 Tap once on the Trash icon to delete the selected message(s)

...cont'd

Whole conversations can also be deleted:

 From a conversation, tap once on the **Back** button to view all of your conversations

 Tap once on the **Edit** button

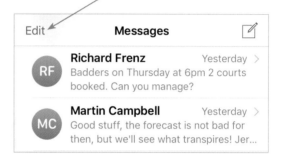

3 Tap once next to any whole conversation(s) that you want to delete

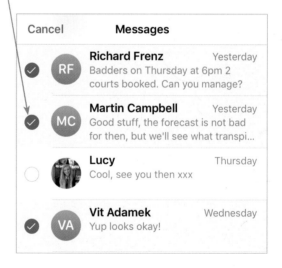

4 Tap once on the **Delete** button at the bottom right-hand corner of the screen to remove the selected conversation(s)

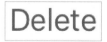

6 The Online World

This chapter shows how to use your iPhone to keep ahead in the fast-moving world of online communications, using the web, email, social media, and video calls.

Getting Online

Connecting to Wi-Fi is one of the main ways that the iPhone can get online access. You will need to have an Internet Service Provider and a Wi-Fi router to connect to the internet. Once this is in place, you will be able to connect to a Wi-Fi network:

You can also get online access through your cellular network, which is provided by your phone network supplier. However, data charges may apply for this.

If you are connecting to your home Wi-Fi network, the iPhone should connect automatically each time, after it has been set up. If you are connecting in a public Wi-Fi area, you will be asked which network you would like to join.

1 Tap once on the **Settings** app

Settings

2 Tap once on the **Wi-Fi** tab

Wi-Fi   Not Connected >

3 Ensure the **Wi-Fi** button is in the **On** position

< Settings   Wi-Fi

Wi-Fi

CHOOSE A NETWORK...

4 Available networks are shown here. Tap once on one to select it

PlusnetWireless792287   🔒 📶 ⓘ

virginmedia6249958   🔒 📶 ⓘ

Other...

5 Enter a password for your Wi-Fi router

Enter the password for "PlusnetWireless792287"

Cancel   **Enter Password**   Join

Password   •••••••••

6 Tap once on the **Join** button   Join

7 Once a network has been joined, a tick appears next to it. This now provides access to the internet

< Settings   Wi-Fi

Wi-Fi

✓ PlusnetWireless792287   🔒 📶 ⓘ

Safari Settings

Safari is the default web browser on the iPhone, and it can be used to bring the web to your iPhone. Before you start using Safari, there are a range of settings that can be applied:

 1 Tap once on the **Settings** app

2 Tap once on the **Safari** tab

3 Make selections under the **Search** section for the default search engine, options for suggestions appearing as you type search words and phrases, and preloading the top-rating page in a search

4 Make selections under the **General** section for entering passwords, specifying the items for the Favorites window, and blocking pop-ups

5 Make selections under the **Privacy & Security** section for blocking cookies, warning about fraudulent websites, checking to see whether websites accept Apple Pay, and clearing your web browsing history and web data

Because of the proliferation of apps available for the iPhone, you may find that you use Safari less than on a desktop or laptop computer. For example, most major news outlets have their own apps that can be used as stand-alone items, rather than having to use Safari to access the site. Look for apps for your favorite websites in the App Store, as a shortcut for accessing them quickly.

Hot tip

The latest iPhones have a setting for **Show Tab Bar**, which displays the open tabs along the top of the Safari window, if the iPhone is being used in landscape mode.

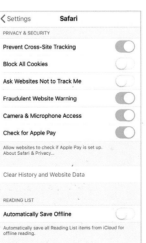

Web Browsing with Safari

To start browsing the web with Safari and enjoy the variety of the information within it:

Don't forget

The **Share** button in Step 5 can be used to share a web page via Message, Mail or social media sites such as Facebook or Twitter. It can also be used to add a web page link to a Note.

 Tap once on the **Safari** app

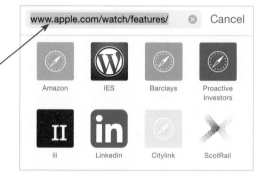 Enter a website address here in the Address Bar, or tap once on one of the items in the Favorites window

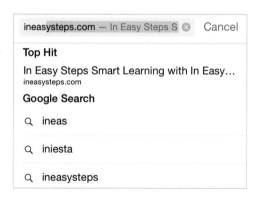 As you type in the Address Bar, website suggestions appear, and also search suggestions with Google

 When you access a web page, use these buttons to visit the Next and Previous pages

 Use this button to share a web page

Use this button to view bookmarks

Use this button to view, add and delete tabs (see pages 112-113)

Adding bookmarks

Everyone has favorite websites that they visit, and in Safari it is possible to mark these with bookmarks so that they can be accessed quickly. To do this:

 Tap once on this button on the bottom toolbar

 Tap once on the **Add Bookmark** button

 Select a name and location for the bookmark, and tap once on the **Save** button

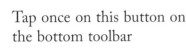

 Tap once on the **Bookmarks** button, and tap once here to view your bookmarks

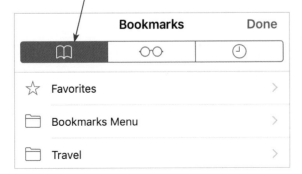

Hot tip

If the bottom toolbar is not visible on a web page, swipe downwards on the page to view it.

Don't forget

The **Bookmarks** button in Step 4 can also be used to access any Reading List items that have been stored. These are added from the **Share** button in Step 1, and enable items to be saved and read later, even if you are not connected to the internet. (The third button in Step 4 is for accessing your web browsing history.)

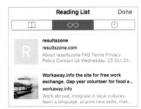

Using Tabs in Safari

In keeping with most modern web browsers, Safari uses tabs so that you can have several websites open at the same time. However, due to the fact that a smartphone's screen is smaller than those on a desktop or laptop computer, tabs operate in a specific way on the iPhone. To use tabs:

Hot tip

Press and hold on a tab to drag it into a different position in Tab View.

Press and hold the Tab button to get the option to close all open tabs in one go.

Don't forget

Tap once on the **Done** button at the bottom of the Tab View window to exit this and return to the web page that was being viewed when Tab View was activated.

1 Open Safari and open a website. Tap once on this button on the bottom toolbar to view all currently open tabs

2 Swipe up and down in Tab View to view all of the open tabs. Tap once on one to view that web page at full size

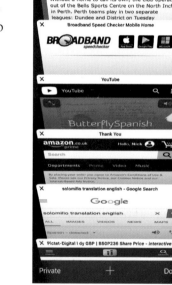

3 Swipe to the bottom of the page to view any tabs that you have open on any other Apple devices, such as an iPad

Opening tabs

To open more tabs in Safari on your iPhone:

 Open the Tab View window as shown opposite, and tap once on this button

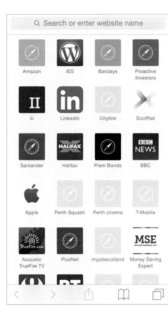 Open the new tab by entering a web address in the Address Bar, or by tapping once on one of the items in the Favorites window

The items that appear in the Favorites window can be specified with the Safari settings: **Settings** > **Safari** > **Favorites** and by then selecting a category. This page will appear when a new tab is opened, and also when you tap in the Address Bar to enter a web address.

 Tap once on the **Private** button in Tab View to open a new tab that is not recorded in your web history

 Open the private tab in the same way as a regular one. This is  indicated by a dark bar at the top of the window

 Tap once on this button to close any tab in Tab View

113

Setting up an Email Account

Email accounts
Email settings can be specified within the Settings app. Different email accounts can also be added there.

1 Tap once on the **Settings** app

2 Tap once on the **Passwords & Accounts** tab

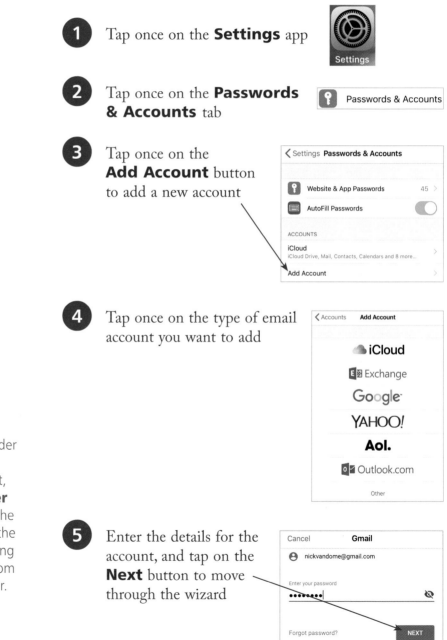

3 Tap once on the **Add Account** button to add a new account

4 Tap once on the type of email account you want to add

Hot tip

If your email provider is not on the **Add Account** list, tap once on **Other** at the bottom of the list and complete the account details using the information from your email provider.

5 Enter the details for the account, and tap on the **Next** button to move through the wizard

...cont'd

 6 Drag these buttons **On** or **Off** to specify which functions are to be available for the required account. Tap once on the **Save** button

7 Each new account is added under the **Accounts** heading of the Mail section

If you set up more than one email account, messages from all of them can be downloaded and displayed by **Mail**.

Email settings

Email settings can be specified within the Settings app:

1 Under the **Mail** section there are several options for how Mail operates and looks. These include how much of an email will be previewed in your Inbox, and options for accessing actions by swiping on an email

The **Organize by Thread** option can be turned **On** to show connected email conversations within your Inbox. If there is a thread of emails, this is indicated by this symbol.

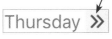

Tap on it once to view the thread.

Emailing

Email on the iPhone is created, sent and received using the Mail app (although other email apps can be downloaded from the App Store). This provides a range of functionality for managing emails and responding to them.

Accessing Mail

To access Mail and start sending and receiving emails:

Hot tip

Use these buttons at the top of the window when you are reading an email to view the Next and Previous messages.

Don't forget

If the **Fetch New Data** option in the **Passwords & Accounts** section is set to **Push**, new emails will be downloaded automatically from your mail server. To check manually, swipe down from the top of the mailbox pane. The Push option uses up more battery power.

1 Tap once on the **Mail** app (the red icon in the corner displays the number of unread emails in your Inbox)

2 Tap once on a message to display it in the main panel

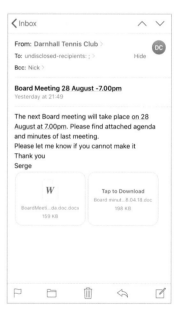

3 Use these buttons to, from left to right, flag a message, move a message to a specific folder, delete a message, respond to a message, and create a new message

4 Tap once on this button to reply to a message, reply to everyone in a conversation, forward it to a new recipient, or print it

Reply
Reply All
Forward
Print
Cancel

To delete an email from your Inbox, swipe on it from right to left, and tap once on the **Trash/Delete** button.

Creating email

To create and send an email:

1 Tap once on this button to create a new message

2 Enter a recipient name in the **To:** box

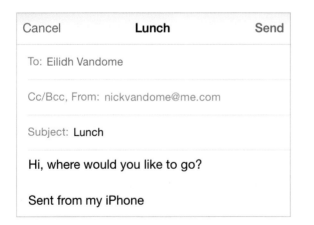

Cancel	**Lunch**	Send

To: Eilidh Vandome

Cc/Bcc, From: nickvandome@me.com

Subject: Lunch

Hi, where would you like to go?

Sent from my iPhone

3 Enter a subject and body text

4 Tap once on the **Send** button to send the email to the recipient

Press and hold in the body text area to get the option to **Insert Photo or Video** to your email. Photos can also be attached to an email by opening them in the **Photos** app, tapping once on the **Share** button and selecting the **Mail** option.

If the recipient is included in your Contacts app, their details will appear as you type in Step 2. Tap once on the email address, if it appears, to include it in the **To:** field of a new email.

117

To make video calls with FaceTime you need an active internet connection and to be signed in with your Apple ID.

Hot tip

The contacts for FaceTime calls are taken from the iPhone Contacts app. You can also add new contacts directly to the contacts list by tapping once on the **+** sign and adding the relevant details for the new contact.

Don't forget

Skype is another option for making free video calls to other Skype users. The app can be downloaded from the App Store.

Having a Video Chat

Video chatting is a very personal and interactive way to keep in touch with family and friends around the world. The FaceTime app provides this facility with other iPhone, iPad and iPod Touch users, or a Mac computer with FaceTime. To use FaceTime for video chatting:

 Tap once on the **FaceTime** app

 Tap once on this button to start a new video chat and tap once here to select a contact

3 Tap once on a contact to access their details for making a FaceTime call

4 Tap once on their phone number or email address to make a FaceTime call. The recipient must have FaceTime on their iPhone, iPad, iPod Touch or Mac computer. Tap once on these buttons next to a contact to make a video or audio call

5 Once you have selected a contact, FaceTime starts connecting to them and displays this at the top of the screen

6 When you have connected, your contact appears in the main window and you appear in a picture-in-picture thumbnail in the corner

7 Tap once on this button to access effects options that can be added to your own video display, including filters and text

Tap once on this button in Step 8 to access any animojis or memojis that you have created (see pages 97-98). Tap once on one to superimpose it over your own face in the FaceTime window. This is a new feature in iOS 12.

8 Tap once on this button to access additional options, including accessing the effects options, flipping the camera view, muting the conversation, putting the conversation on speaker, and turning the camera off

9 Tap once on this button to end a FaceTime call

119

Adding Social Media

Using social media sites such as Facebook, Twitter, and Snapchat to keep in touch with family and friends has now become common across all generations. On the iPhone with iOS 12, it is possible to link to these accounts so that you can share content to them from your iPhone, and also view updates through the Notification Center. To add social media apps to your iPhone:

Hot tip

Updates can be set to appear in your **Notification Center**. Open **Settings**, and tap once on the **Notifications** tab. Under the **Notification Style** heading, tap once on the social media site and select options for how you would like the notifications to appear.

1 Open the App Store and navigate to the **Apps** > **Categories** > **Social Networking** section

 Social Networking

2 Tap once on the required apps to download them to your iPhone

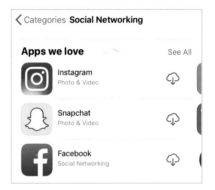

< Categories **Social Networking**

Apps we love   See All

Instagram
Photo & Video

Snapchat
Photo & Video

Facebook
Social Networking

3 Tap once on an app to open it

Don't forget

Social media sites can be accessed from their own apps on the iPhone, and also from their respective websites, using Safari.

4 If you already have an account with the social media service, enter your login details, or tap once on the **Sign Up** button to create a new account

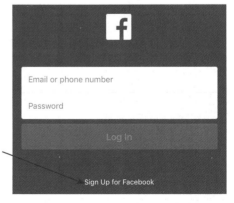

Email or phone number

Password

Log In

Sign Up for Facebook

7 Hands on with Apps

Apps are the items that give the iPhone its functionality. This chapter details the pre-installed apps, and also shows how to access those in the App Store.

You need an active internet connection to download apps from the App Store.

Within a number of apps there is a **Share** button that can be used to share items through a variety of methods, including iMessages, email, Facebook and Twitter.

What is an App?

An app is just a more modern name for a computer program. Initially, it was used in relation to mobile devices such as the iPhone and the iPad, but it is now becoming more widely used with desktop and laptop computers, for both Mac and Windows operating systems.

On the iPhone there are two types of apps:

- **Pre-installed apps**. These are the apps that come already installed on the iPhone.

- **App Store apps**. These are apps that can be downloaded from the online App Store. There is a huge range of apps available there, covering a variety of different categories. Some are free, while others have to be paid for. The apps in the App Store are updated and added to on a daily basis, so there are always new ones to explore.

There are also two important points about apps (both pre-installed and those from the App Store) to remember:

- Apart from some of the pre-installed apps, the majority of apps do not interact with each other. This means that there is less chance of viruses being transmitted from app to app on your iPhone, and they can operate without a reliance on other apps.

- Content created by apps is saved within the app itself, rather than within a file structure on your iPhone; e.g. if you create a note in the Notes app, it is saved there; if you take a photo, it is saved in the Photos app. Content is usually also saved automatically when it is created or edited, so you do not have to worry about saving it as you work on it.

Pre-installed Apps

The pre-installed iPhone apps are the ones that appear on the Home screen when you first get your iPhone:

- **App Store**. This can be used to access the online App Store, from where additional apps can be downloaded and updated.

- **Books**. This is an app for downloading electronic books, which can then be read on the iPhone.

- **Calculator**. This is a basic calculator, which can also be accessed from the Control Center.

- **Calendar**. An app for storing appointments, important dates, and other calendar information. It can be synced with iCloud.

- **Camera**. This gives direct access to the front-facing and rear-facing iPhone cameras.

- **Clock**. This displays the current time, and can be used to view the time in different countries. It also has an alarm clock and a stopwatch.

- **Compass**. This can be used to show you the direction of North. You can give the compass access to your location so that you can follow it from where you are.

- **Contacts**. An address book app. Once contacts are added here they can then also be accessed from other apps, such as Mail.

- **FaceTime**. This app uses the front-facing FaceTime camera to hold video or audio chats with compatible Apple devices.

- **Files**. This is used to back up items and make them available to other Apple devices.

Hot tip

Some of the default apps are located on the second Home screen, within the **Extras** folder.

Hot tip

If you don't want your contacts to be accessed by other apps then open **Settings** > **Privacy** > **Contacts** and drag the button for these apps to **Off**, if any appear here.

...cont'd

- **Find Friends**. This can be used to view the location of family and friends, based on their Apple mobile devices and Mac computers.

- **Find iPhone**. This can be used to locate your iPhone and other Apple devices. It is set up in **Settings** > **iCloud**.

- **Health**. This stores and collates a range of health information. See pages 137-138.

- **Home**. This is a new app in iOS 12 that can be used to control certain compatible functions within the home, such as heating controls.

- **iTunes Store**. This app can be used to browse the iTunes Store, where content can be downloaded to your iPhone.

- **Mail**. This is the email app for sending and receiving email on your iPhone.

- **Maps**. Use this app to view maps from around the world, find specific locations, and get directions to destinations.

- **Measure**. This can be used to measure the length or perimeter of items.

- **Messages**. This is the iPhone messaging service, which can be used for SMS text messages and iMessages between compatible Apple devices.

- **Music**. An app for playing music on your iPhone and also viewing cover artwork. You can also use it to create your own playlists.

- **News**. This collates news stories from numerous online publications and categories.

- **Notes**. If you need to jot down your thoughts or ideas, this app is perfect for just that.

You need an Apple ID to obtain content from the iTunes Store and Books.

The Measure app is a new app in iOS 12 (see page 141).

- **Photos**. This is an app for viewing and editing your photos and videos, and creating slideshows. It can also be used to share photos.

- **Podcasts**. This can be used to download podcasts from within the App Store.

A podcast is an audio or video program, and they cover an extensive range of subjects.

- **Reminders**. Use this app to help keep organized, when you want to create to-do lists and set reminders for events.

- **Safari**. The Apple web browser that has been developed for viewing the web on your iPhone.

- **Settings**. This contains a range of settings for the iPhone (see pages 20-21 for details).

- **Stocks**. Use this to display the latest stock market prices and add your own companies.

- **Tips**. This can be used to display tips and hints for items on your iPhone.

- **TV**. This is an app for viewing videos from the iTunes Store, and also streaming them to a larger HDTV monitor.

- **Voice Memos**. This can be used to record short audio reminders that can be stored and played on the iPhone.

- **Wallet**. This can be used to store credit, debit, and storecard details, for making payments with Apple Pay (in some locations).

- **Watch**. This can be used to pair an iPhone with the Apple Watch and apply a range of settings.

- **Weather**. Displays weather details for your location and destinations around the world.

About the App Store

While the pre-installed apps that come with the iPhone are flexible and versatile, apps really come into their own when you connect to the App Store. This is an online resource, and there are thousands of apps there that can be downloaded and then used on your iPhone, including categories from Lifestyle to Medical and Travel.

To use the App Store, you must first have an Apple ID. This can be obtained when you first connect to the App Store. Once you have an Apple ID, you can start exploring the App Store and the apps within it:

The design of the App Store has been enhanced in iOS 12.

126

Don't forget

The items within the Today section of the App Store change on a regular basis, so it is always worth looking at it from time to time.

1 Tap once on the **App Store** app on the Home screen

App Store

2 The latest available apps are displayed on the Homepage of the App Store, including the featured and best new apps

3 Tap on these buttons to view items according to **Today**, **Games**, **Apps**, and **Updates**

Viewing apps

To view apps in the App Store and read about their content and functionality:

1 Tap once on an app

2 General details about the app are displayed

3 Swipe left or right here to view additional information about the app, and view details

4 Scroll down the page to see additional information including reviews and new items in this version of the app

Don't forget

If it is an upgraded version of an app, this page will include details of any fixes and improvements that have been made.

Don't forget

Some apps will differ depending on the geographical location from which you are accessing the App Store.

Hot tip

There is an increasing number of AR (Augmented Reality) apps in the App Store. These are apps that combine real-life images, either within the app or from the device's camera, that are used with graphical elements; e.g. constellations can be drawn over an image of the sky in an astronomy app.

Finding Apps

Featured

Within the App Store, apps are separated into categories according to type. This enables you to find apps according to particular subjects. To do this:

1 Tap once on the **Apps** button on the toolbar at the bottom of the App Store

2 Scroll up and down to view all of the sections within the Apps Homepage, and scroll left and right to view items within each section heading

3 Scroll down the page to the **Top Categories** section, and tap once on the **See All** button to view the full range of categories of apps

Top Categories	See All
AR Apps	
Health & Fitness	
Entertainment	
Kids	
Lifestyle	
Shopping	

4 Tap once on a category to view the items within it. This can be navigated in the same way as the main Homepage in the App Store; e.g. swipe up and down to view sections, and left and right on each panel to view the available apps

Top Charts

To find the top-rated apps:

 Tap once on the **Apps** button on the toolbar at the bottom of the App Store

 Scroll down the page to view the **Top Paid** and **Top Free** apps

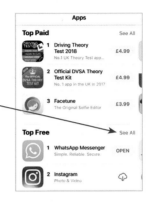

Tap once on the **See All** button to view all of the Top Paid or Top Charts apps

Do not limit yourself to just viewing the top apps. Although these are the most popular, there are also a lot of excellent apps within each category.

Searching for apps

Another way to find apps is with the App Store Search box, which appears at the top of the App Store window once it has been accessed. To use this to find apps:

 Tap once on the **Search** button at the bottom of the window to access the Search box

Tap in the Search box to activate the keyboard and enter a search keyword or phrase

For more information about using the iPhone virtual keyboard, see Chapter 5.

Suggested apps appear as you are typing

Tap on an app to view it

Downloading Apps

When you identify an app that you would like to use, it can be downloaded to your iPhone. To do this:

Apps usually download in a few minutes or less, depending on the speed of your Wi-Fi connection.

1 Find the app you want, using the **App Store**

2 Tap once on the **Price** or **Get** button

Some apps have "in-app purchases". This is additional content that has to be paid for when it is downloaded.

3 Tap once on the **Install** button

4 The app is downloaded to the next available space on the Home screen

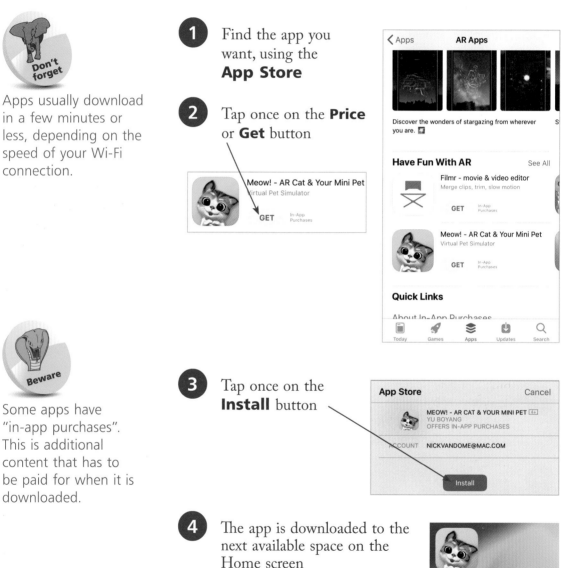

Updating Apps

The publishers of apps provide updates that bring new features and improvements. You do not have to check your apps to see if there are updates – you can set them to be updated automatically through the Settings app. To do this:

1 Open **Settings** and tap on the **iTunes & App Store** tab

	iTunes & App Store	>

Settings

	Siri & Search	>
	Touch ID & Passcode	>
SOS	Emergency SOS	>
	Battery	>
	Privacy	>
	iTunes & App Store	>
	Wallet & Apple Pay	>
	Passwords & Accounts	>
	Mail	>
	Contacts	>
	Calendar	>
	Notes	>

Hot tip

You should keep your apps as up-to-date as possible to take advantage of software fixes and any updates to the iPhone operating system (iOS).

131

2 Drag the **Updates** button under **Automatic Downloads** to **On** to enable automatic updates for apps

	Updates	

< Settings   **iTunes & App Stores**

Apple ID: nickvandome@mac.com

Password Settings   >

AUTOMATIC DOWNLOADS

	Music	
	Apps	
	Books & Audiobooks	
	Updates	

Automatically download new purchases (including free) made on other devices.

Use Cellular Data

Use cellular network for automatic downloads.

Video Autoplay   On >

Automatically play app preview videos in the App Store.

Managing your Apps

As more apps are added it can become hard to find the ones you want, particularly if you have to swipe between several screens. However, it is possible to organize apps into individual folders to make using them more manageable. To do this:

Hot tip

Folders are an excellent way to manage your apps, and ensure that you do not have numerous Home screens cluttered up with different apps.

Hot tip

Folders can also be added to the Dock after you have created them, enabling several apps to be stored here.

 Press on an app until it starts to jiggle and a cross appears at the top-left corner. (The cross can be used to delete the app – see next page)

2 Drag the app over another one

3 A folder is created, containing the two apps. The folder is given a default name, usually based on the category of the first app

4 Tap once on the folder name and type a new name, if required

5 Tap on the **Done** button on the keyboard to finish creating the folder

 The folder is added on the Home screen. Tap on this to access the items within it (press and hold on it to move it)

Deleting Apps

If you decide that you do not want certain apps anymore, they can be deleted from your iPhone. However, they remain in the iCloud so that you can reinstall them if you change your mind. This also means that if you delete an app by mistake, you can get it back from the App Store without having to pay for it again. To do this:

 Press on an app until it starts to jiggle and a cross appears at the top-left corner

 Tap once on the cross to delete the app. In the Delete dialog box, tap once on the **Delete** button

Delete "Animated Emojis for iMessage"?

Deleting this app will also delete its data.

| Cancel | Delete |

 To reinstall a deleted app, tap once on the **App Store** app

App Store

 Tap once on the **Updates** button on the bottom toolbar

Updates

Beware

If you delete an app it will also delete any data that has been compiled with that app, even if you reinstall it from the App Store.

Hot tip

Most of the pre-installed apps can now be deleted, using iOS 12. The ones that cannot be deleted are: App Store, Camera, Clock, Find iPhone, Health, Messages, Phone, Photos, Safari, Settings, and Wallet.

...cont'd

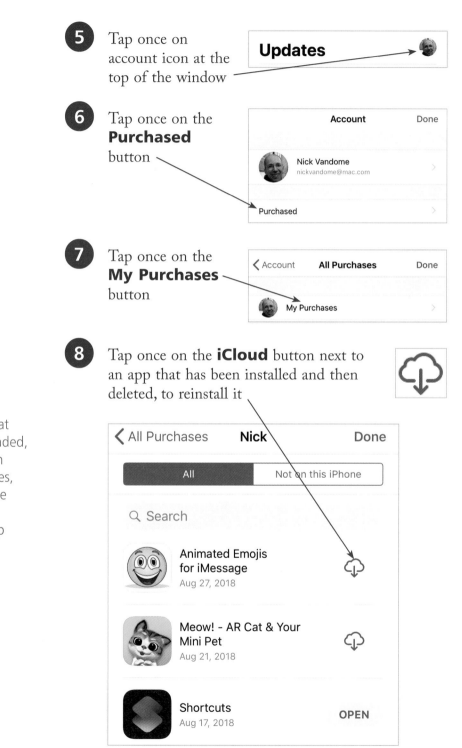

5 Tap once on account icon at the top of the window

Updates

6 Tap once on the **Purchased** button

Account   Done

Nick Vandome
nickvandome@mac.com

Purchased

7 Tap once on the **My Purchases** button

Account   **All Purchases**   Done

My Purchases

8 Tap once on the **iCloud** button next to an app that has been installed and then deleted, to reinstall it

All Purchases   **Nick**   Done

All   Not on this iPhone

Search

Animated Emojis
for iMessage
Aug 27, 2018

Meow! - AR Cat & Your
Mini Pet
Aug 21, 2018

Shortcuts
Aug 17, 2018   OPEN

Don't forget

All of the apps that you have downloaded, including those on other Apple devices, will be listed in the **My Purchases** section of the App Store.

8 Apps for Every Day

The iPhone has apps to make your day-to-day life run more smoothly, including staying healthy, keeping notes, and reading the news.

Don't forget

The Apple Watch has to be used in conjunction with an iPhone 6 (or later) to activate its full range of functionality. It is "paired" with an iPhone using the Watch app.

Don't forget

The App Store also has a **Medical** category.

Beware

If you have a pre-existing medical condition, or are on any medication, always consult your doctor before using a new health or fitness app that could have an impact on this.

Health Options on the iPhone

The Health app

The iPhone has a pre-installed app to assist with a range of areas for health and fitness. This is the Health app, and it can be used to store a range of health information – see pages 137-138 for details.

Working with the Apple Watch

In April 2015 Apple introduced the Apple Watch, and it has now reached its fourth version: Apple Watch 4. This is much more than a watch, though: it is also a body monitoring device. It has a number of sensors on the back, which monitor information such as heart rate and body movement. There is also an activity app to measure your

fitness activities. A lot of this data can be sent to the Health app on the iPhone, where it can be stored and analyzed in greater depth. Wearable technology like the Apple Watch is growing rapidly, and there are likely to be more and more health and fitness features added as this technology evolves.

App Store health and fitness apps

The App Store not only has a wide range of health and fitness apps; it even has a whole category for them:

1 Tap once on the **App Store** app

2 Tap once on the **Apps** button

3 In the categories section, tap once on the **Health & Fitness** category

4 The health and fitness apps are displayed. Scroll down the page to view the **Top Paid** and **Top Free** health and fitness apps

Using the Health App

The Health app is available in iOS 12, and it enables you to input and analyze a wide range of health and fitness information. There are four main areas:

- **Today**. This displays health data that has been collated for specific days.

- **Health Data**. This displays the available categories within the Health app.

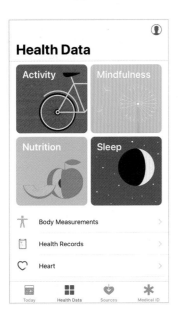

- **Sources**. This displays information from any other health apps on your iPhone, providing they have requested access to the Health app.

- **Medical ID**. This can be used to add your own medical information such as medical conditions, allergies, blood type, and emergency contacts.

New apps designed to interact with the Health app are being produced by a number of different third-party developers.

Tap on the calendar at the top of the Today window to view data from different dates. The current date is indicated by a red circle.

137

Some items in the Health app have data added automatically, such as Walking + Running, Steps, and Flights Climbed, in the Activity category. Other items need to have their data added manually (see page 138).

Don't forget

Here, you get the option to enter your personal data and medical details. It is well worth entering these for emergencies.

Beware

When adding data, do so at regular intervals, otherwise the results and analysis may not be complete.

Don't forget

Once data has been added, it is shown on the graph in Step 4. Add data for more categories, as required.

Hot tip

See **iPhone & Apple Watch for Health & Fitness in easy steps** for more help on using these devices to achieve your health goals.

...cont'd

Adding health data

To enter a range of information into the Health app:

 1 Tap once on the **Health Data** button

 2 Tap once on one of the main categories

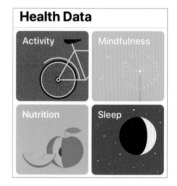

 3 Tap once on one of the sub-categories; e.g. Calcium in the Nutrition category

 4 Tap once on this button to add data for the selected item

 5 Add the data for the selected item, and tap once on the **Add** button

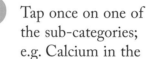

Jotting Down Notes

It is always useful to have a quick way of making notes of everyday things, such as shopping lists, recipes, or packing lists for traveling. On your iPhone, the Notes app is perfect for this function. To use it:

1 Tap once on the **Notes** app

2 Tap once on this button on the bottom toolbar to create a new note

3 Enter text for the note

4 Tap once on this button to share (via Message or Mail, or any social media apps on your iPhone), copy or print a note

5 Tap once on this button to access the formatting toolbar. (Tap once on the cross to close the toolbar)

6 Double-tap on text to select it, and tap once on this button to access text formatting options

If iCloud is turned **On** for Notes (**Settings > Apple ID > iCloud > Notes**) then all of your notes will be stored here and will be available on any other iCloud-enabled devices that you have.

The first line of a note becomes its title when viewed in the list of all notes. (To view this, tap once on the **iCloud** button in Step 3.)

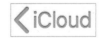

You can edit a note at any time by tapping on it once in the top-level folder and editing the text as required.

...cont'd

Don't forget

For more information about selecting text, see pages 90-91.

Hot tip

Press and hold firmly on the keyboard in Notes to activate it as a trackpad. You can then swipe over it to move the cursor around the screen.

Hot tip

Tap once on the **Scan Documents** button in Step 10 to scan a document into the current note.

Don't forget

Tap once on this icon on the bottom toolbar to delete the current note.

7 Tap once on this button to create a checklist. Add items to the list. Tap once on a check button to add a tick and show it as completed

‹ iCloud Done	‹ iCloud Done
Shopping list	Shopping list
◯ Fruit	◯ Fruit
◯ Pasta	◔ Pasta
◯ Eggs	◯ Eggs

8 Tap once on this button to share the current note by Message, Mail, or a social media app and allow someone else to edit it

9 Tap once on this button to add a handwritten item or drawing

10 Tap once on this button to add a photo or video to a note. Select a photo or video from your library, or take a new one

Scan Documents

Take Photo or Video

Photo Library

Add Sketch

Cancel

11 The latest note appears at the top of the iCloud list. Each time a note is edited, it moves to the top

‹   Edit

iCloud

Handwritten note!
10:39   Handwritten note
🗀 Notes

Club Champs
Yesterday   Men's Singles
🗀 Notes

Measuring Items

The Measure app uses the iPhone's camera to measure the distance between two points, and also the perimeter of each side of objects and areas. To use the Measure app:

1   Tap once on the **Measure** app

2   The Measure app opens the iPhone's camera. Move the iPhone and position the white dot within the circle at the starting point for the measurement. Tap once on the **+** (**Add a point**) button

3   Move the iPhone along the item to be measured (the line is yellow during the measurement). Move the iPhone up or down to change the position of the line

4   Tap once on the **+** button when the white dot reaches the required end point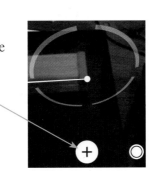

5   The measurement is displayed on a white line, which is the length of the measurement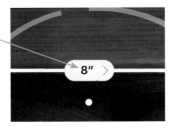

The Measure app is a new item in iOS 12.

Beware

Ensure that there is enough natural light for the camera to work accurately when measuring items.

Don't forget

The Measure app is an example of Augmented Reality (AR). This is when a real life image is superimposed with a graphical element; in this case, the items of measurement.

Hot tip

Position the white dot within the circle over an existing end point of a measurement and tap once on the **+** button to add another measurement.

Keeping Up-to-Date

The Calendar can be used to add events and appointments and keep yourself up-to-date with your daily, monthly, and annual activities.

1 Tap once on the **Calendar** app

2 If **Month** view is displayed, tap once here to access **Year** view. In Year view, tap once on a month to view it

3 Tap once on a day to view it (the current day is highlighted red)

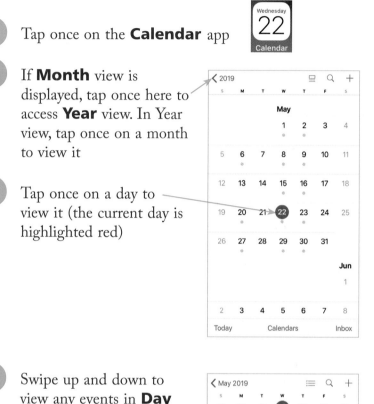

142

4 Swipe up and down to view any events in **Day** view. Tap once on an event to view its details

Adding events

To add new events to the calendar:

1 Press and hold on a time slot within Day view, or tap once on this button

2 Enter a title for the event, and tap once on the **Starts** button to add a start time

3 Add an end time, by tapping on the **Ends** button, and also a repeat frequency (for recurring events such as birthdays). Select a specific calendar for the event and add an alert, if required. Tap once on the **Add** button to create the event

4 Tap once on this button to view a list of your current events and appointments

Drag the **All-day** button to **On** to set an event for the whole day, rather than adding specific start and end times.

The repeat frequency for an event can be set to every day, every week, every 2 weeks, every month, or every year. There is also a **Custom** option for specific time periods.

143

Recording Voice Memos

Voice memos are an increasingly popular way to send short voice messages to family and friends. They can also be used as a method of verbal note-taking when you want to remember something. To use voice memos:

The Voice Memos app has been updated in iOS 12.

Hot tip

If the Voice Memos app is not readily visible, look in the **Utilities** folder on the second Home screen.

Don't forget

Tap once on the menu button, as accessed in Step 5, to **Duplicate** or **Share** a voice memo, in addition to editing a recording.

1 Tap once on the **Voice Memos** app

2 Tap once on the red **Record** button to start recording a voice memo

3 Tap once on this button to finish recording

4 The memo is displayed in the main voice memo window. Tap once on the **Play** button to hear the recording

Voice Memos
Home
16:44   00:03
0:00   -0:03
•••   ⟲15   ▶   ⟳15   🗑

5 Tap once here and tap once on the **Edit Recording** button to amend the existing voice memo

Edit Recording

6 Tap once on this button in the top right-hand corner of the record window to trim the existing voice memo

7 Drag the yellow borders of a recording to trim its start and end points. Tap once on the **Trim** button to edit the recording

Trim

8 Tap once on the **Save** button to save the amended recording

Getting the News

The iPhone with iOS 12 is ideal for keeping up with the news, whether you are on the move or at home. This is made even easier with the News app, which can be used to collate news stories from numerous online media outlets, covering hundreds of subjects. To use it:

1 Tap once on the **News** app

2 Tap once on the **Today** button on the bottom toolbar to view the latest stories in your news feed

3 Tap once on the **More Top Stories** link to view the top items recommended by Apple News (based on your own news selections)

4 Tap once on the **Channels** button on the bottom toolbar to view subjects or publications that you are following; i.e. they are used to populate your news feed

NEW

The layout of the News app has been updated in iOS 12.

Hot tip

To delete an item from the Following section on the Channels page, tap once on the **Edit** button in the top right-hand corner and tap on the red circle next to the item you want to delete. This will remove its related content from your news feed.

...cont'd

Hot tip

Tap once the **Spotlight** button on the bottom toolbar to view in-depth articles on subjects selected by Apple News.

Spotlight

Hot tip

When an article has been opened for reading (by tapping once on it on the Today page), tap once on this button at the top of the window to increase the text size.

5 Under the **Suggested by Siri** heading, tap once on a heart icon to include that subject or publication in your news feed

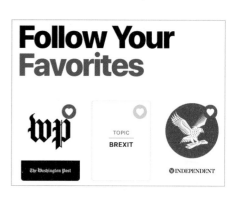

6 Scroll down the main Channels page and tap once on the **Discover Channels & Topics** button to add more subjects or publications

PERSONALIZE YOUR NEWS
Follow your favorite channels and topics to improve your reading experience.

Discover Channels & Topics

7 Tap once on an item to add it to your Favorites (so it will show up in your news feed) and tap once on the **Done** button at the bottom of the window

Follow Your Favorites

wp   TOPIC BREXIT   INDEPENDENT
The Washington Post

Done

8 When an article has been opened for reading,

tap on these buttons on the bottom toolbar to, from left to right: share the item (or save it); follow a news topic for more similar items; or unfollow a news topic so you see fewer items

9 Relaxing with your iPhone

This chapter shows how to get the most out of your iPhone for playing music and reading, and also how to shop and research online.

Around the iTunes Store

The iPhone performs an excellent role as a mobile entertainment center: its versatility means that you can carry your music, videos, and books in your pocket. Most of this content comes from the online iTunes Store. To access this and start adding content to your iPhone:

1 Tap once on the **iTunes Store** app

2 The iTunes Store interface is similar to the App Store. Tap once on the **Featured** or **Charts** tabs at the top of the window to view these headings

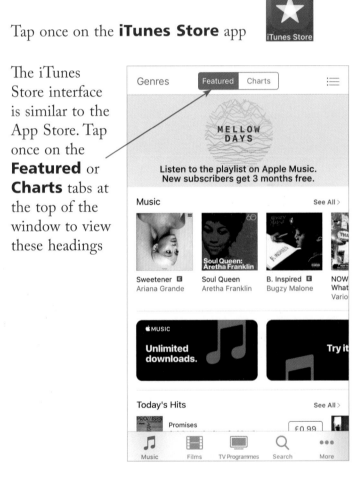

Tap once on the **Genres** button at the top of the Music Homepage to view items for different musical genres and styles.

Genres

Tap once on the **Charts** tab at the top of the iTunes Store window to view the top-ranking items for the category that is being viewed.

Charts

3 Use the buttons on the bottom toolbar to access content for Music, Films/Movies and TV Programmes/Shows

4 Swipe to the left and right on each panel to view items within it

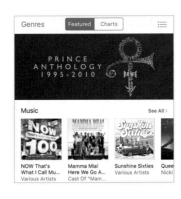

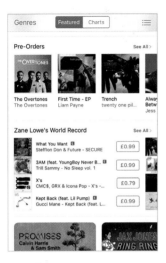

5 Swipe up and down to view more headings

Downloaded movies and TV shows take up a lot of storage space on the iPhone.

6 Tap once on the **Films/Movies** button to view the movies in the iTunes Store. These can be bought or rented

7 Tap once on the **TV Programmes/Shows** button to view the TV shows in the iTunes Store. These can be bought or rented

To view all of your iTunes purchases, tap once on the **More** button on the bottom toolbar and tap once on the **Purchased** button. View your purchases by category (Music, Films/Movies or TV Programmes/ Shows), and tap once on the cloud symbol next to a purchased item to download it to your iPhone.

8 Tap once on the **More** button to access additional content

●●●
More

9 Tap once on the **Genius** button to view suggested content, based on what you have already bought from the iTunes Store

More	Edit
🔔 Tones	>
⚛ Genius	>
♪ Purchased	>
⬇ Downloads	>

Buying Items

Once you have found the content you want in the iTunes Store, you can then buy it and download it to your iPhone.

Don't forget

If you have set up Apple Pay (see pages 54-55) you will be able to use this to buy items in the iTunes Store. Use the Face ID function – see page 24 – (or Touch ID for older iPhones with iOS 12) in Step 1, after you have tapped on the price button, to authorize the payment using Apple Pay.

1 For music items, tap once on the price button next to an item (either an album or individual songs) and follow the instructions. Tap once on the **Music** app to play the item (see next page)

⟨ Music		⬆

Soul Queen
Aretha Franklin ⟩

R&B/Soul
60 Songs
Released Oct 29, 2007
★★★★★ (41)   £9.99

Songs	Reviews	Related

1	I Never Loved a Man (The Way I Love You)	2:44	£0.99
2	Do Right Woman, Do Right Man	3:16	£0.99
3	Save Me	2:16	£0.99
4	Drown In My Own Tears	4:03	£0.99
5	Baby, Baby, Baby	2:53	£0.99

Music

2 For movies and TV shows, tap once on the **Buy** or **Rent** button next to the title. Tap once on the **TV** app to play the item

TV

Don't forget

For rented movies and TV shows, you have 30 days to watch an item after you have downloaded it. After you have started watching, you have 48 hours until it expires.

⟨ Films

Peter Rabbit
PG

£13.99 BUY
£4.49 RENT

(104)

4K   DOLBY VISION   CC

iTunes Extras — Included with 4K film purchase.

Details	Reviews	Related

Playing Music

Once music has been bought from the iTunes Store, it can be played on your iPhone using the Music app. To do this:

Tap once on the **Music** app

Tap once on the **Library** button on the bottom toolbar

Select one of the options for viewing items in the Library. This can be **Playlists**, **Artists**, **Albums**, **Songs**, and **Downloaded Music**

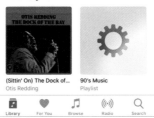

To create a playlist of songs, tap once on the **Playlists** button in Step 3, then tap once on the **New Playlist...** button. Give it a name and then add songs from your Library, using the **Add Music** button.

For the **Artists** section, tap once on an artist to view details of their songs on your iPhone

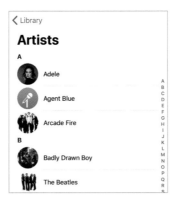

...cont'd

 5 Select a track
to play it

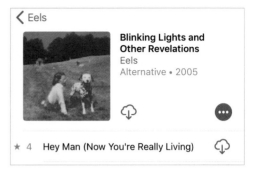

Don't
forget

Tap once on
this button in
Step 5 to access
a menu for the current
track. This includes
options to download
the track, delete it
from the Music app
Library, add it to a
playlist, or share it.

6 A limited
version of the
music controls
appears at the
bottom of the
window

7 Tap once here
to view the full
version of the
music controls.
Use these buttons
to return to
the start of a
track, play/pause
a track, fast-
forward, and
adjust the volume

Don't
forget

By default, music that
has been bought from
the iTunes Store is
kept online and can
be played on your
iPhone by streaming it
over Wi-Fi. However,
it is also possible
to download tracks
to your iPhone so
that you can play
them without being
online. Tap once on
this button to
download a
specific track.

Using Apple Music

Apple Music is a service that makes the entire Apple iTunes Library of music available to users. It is a subscription service, but there is a three-month free trial. Music can be streamed over the internet or downloaded so you can listen to it when you are offline. To start with Apple Music:

1 Tap once on the **Music** app

2 Tap once on the **For You** button

3 Tap once on the **Choose Your Plan** button. (This option is available if you have already used the free, three-month trial of Apple Music)

4 Select the type of plan to which you want to subscribe, and tap once on the **Join Apple Music** button. Once you have joined Apple Music, you will be able to select the music genres in which you are most interested and receive suggestions based on this. You will also be able to listen to the entire iTunes Library of music

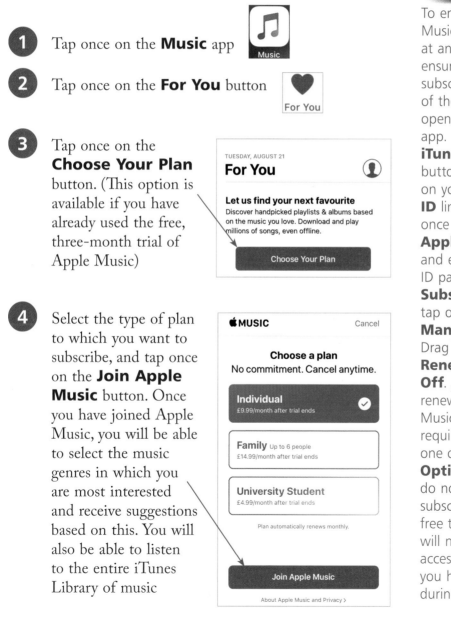

Hot tip

To end your Apple Music subscription at any point (and to ensure you do not subscribe at the end of the free trial), open the **Settings** app. Tap once on the **iTunes & App Store** button, and tap once on your own **Apple ID** link (in blue). Tap once on the **View Apple ID** button and enter your Apple ID password. Under **Subscriptions**, tap once on the **Manage** button. Drag the **Automatic Renewal** button to **Off**. You can then renew your Apple Music membership, if required, by selecting one of the **Renewal Options**. If you do not renew your subscription once the free trial finishes, you will not be able to access any music that you have downloaded during the trial.

Reading

In addition to audio and visual content from the iTunes Store, it is also possible to read books on your iPhone using the Books app (formerly iBooks). To do this:

 Tap once on the **Books** app

 Tap once on the **Reading Now** button on the bottom toolbar to view any items you have in your Library

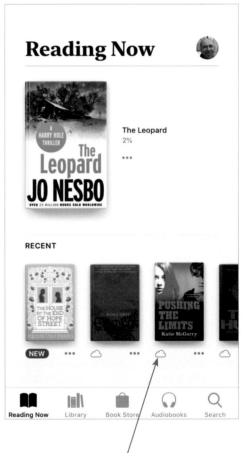

 If a title has a cloud icon next to it, tap once on this to download the book to your iPhone

4 Tap once on the **Library** button

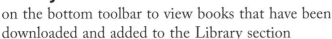

on the bottom toolbar to view books that have been downloaded and added to the Library section

5 Tap once on a title to open it for reading. Tap once here to access options for browsing collections within the Library; e.g. looking for books in certain categories such as Crime and Romance

Hot tip

If you have a Kindle account, you can download the Kindle app from the App Store and use this to connect to your account and all of the books within it.

Kindle
Read eBooks & Magazines
★★★★★ 52.6K

6 Tap once on the **Book Store** button on the bottom toolbar to view books in the Book Store

Book Store

155

Don't forget

Once books have been downloaded to your iPhone, tap once on a title in the **Library** section to read it. Tap on the left or right of the screen to move between pages, or swipe from the left or right edges. Tap in the middle of a page to activate the reading controls at the top of the screen, including Table of Contents, text size, and color options.

Shopping

Online shopping was one of the first great commercial successes on the web. Thousands of retailers now have their own websites and, increasingly, their own apps that can be used on the iPhone. So there are now more options than ever for online shopping:

Don't forget

For some online retailers, you will have to register and create an account before you can buy items. For others, you will be able to go straight to the checkout and enter your payment details.

Don't forget

A number of online retailers offer Apple Pay (see pages 54-55) as a method of payment, denoted by the Apple Pay logo. The number of retailers offering this is likely to grow considerably as Apple Pay becomes more widely available.

 Download apps from the App Store for well-known retailers such as Amazon and eBay

 Use Safari and look up the retailer's website (in some cases, the website will have an option to download the app too)

Some websites will only enable you to download the retailer's app and use this

Comparing prices

Online retailing has also made it a lot easier to compare prices between sites. This can be done in two main ways:

1 Use Safari and search for price comparison websites. Different sites specialize in different products and services, so you may want to use a number of them

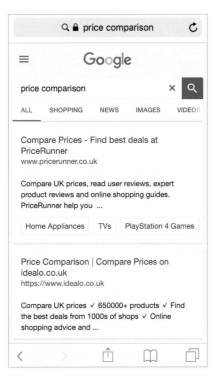

Hot tip

Another option for comparing prices is to check them in a bricks-and-mortar shop, and then compare them with the online prices.

157

2 There are apps in the App Store that can be used to scan barcodes of products and then compare prices for a specific item across different retailers

Researching

With your iPhone in your hand, you literally have a world of information at your fingertips. Whatever your hobby or interest, you will be able to find out a lot more about it using several different options:

1 Press and hold on the **On/Off** button (or the **Home** button for older iPhones) to access **Siri** and make an enquiry this way

2 Use the **App Store** to search for apps for your chosen subject

Don't forget

By default, the search engine used by Safari is Google. However, this can be changed in **Settings** > **Safari** > **Search Engine**.

3 Search **Safari** to find related websites and also general information about a specific topic

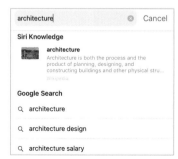

10 On the Go

The iPhone is a great companion whenever you are out and about anywhere, whether at home or abroad.

Finding Locations

Finding locations around the world is only ever a couple of taps away when you have your iPhone and the Maps app.

The Maps app works best if you have Location Services turned on, so that it can show your current location and give directions in relation to this. To turn on Location Services, go to **Settings** > **Privacy** > **Location Services** > **Maps** and tap once on **While Using the App**.

When you tap in the Maps Search box it expands towards the top of the screen.

1 Tap once on the **Maps** app

2 The Search box is at the bottom of the window

3 Enter an item into the Search box. As you type, suggestions appear underneath. Tap on one to go to that location

4 For the current location, options for searching over items such as food outlets, shops, and entertainment are available. Tap on one of these to see results for these categories in the current location

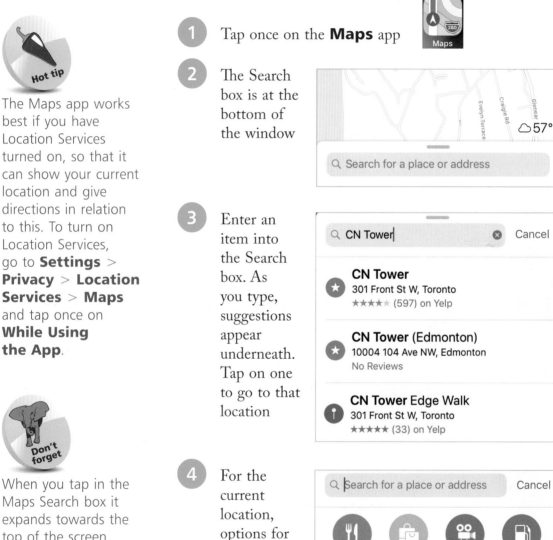

5 The location selected in Step 3 is displayed, with information about it at the bottom of the window

Some locations, such as airports and shopping centers, can display indoor layouts.

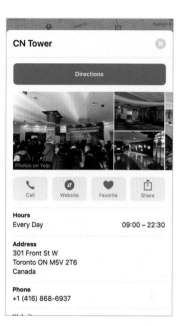

6 Swipe up from the bottom of the window to view full details about the location, including photos, address, phone number, and website address, if available

Some locations have a 3D Flyover Tour feature. This is an automated tour of a location, featuring its most notable sites. It covers major cities around the world, and the list is regularly being added to. If it is available for a location, tap once on the **Flyover** button at the bottom of the window, next to the **Directions** button. Tap once on the **Start City Tour** button to start the Flyover Tour. Try it with a location such as New York, London or Paris.

7 At the top of the Maps app window, tap once on this icon for map style options

8 Select either **Standard (Map)**, **Transit** or **Satellite** to view the map in that style

Getting Directions

Wherever you are in the world, you can get directions between two locations. To do this:

Hot tip

You can enter the Start point as your current location. Tap once on this button to view your current location.

Beware

If you enter the name of a landmark you may also be shown other items that have the same name, such as businesses.

Hot tip

For some destinations, alternative routes will be displayed, depending on distance and traffic conditions. Tap once on the alternative route to select it. Directions for each route can be selected at the bottom of the window.

1 Tap once in the Search box at the bottom of the window in the Maps app

2 Enter the destination (by default, this is from your current location)

3 Tap once on the **Directions** button. The route is shown on the map

4 Tap once on these buttons at the bottom of the window to view the route for **Drive**, **Walk**, **Transit**, or a taxi **Ride** using an appropriate app

5 Tap once on the **Go** button to view step-by-step instructions on the map

6 The route is displayed, from your starting location. Audio instructions tell you the directions to be followed. You can use the volume buttons (on the side of the iPhone) to increase or decrease the sound. As you follow the route, the map and instructions are updated

The arrow in Step 6 points in the current direction of travel; i.e. the direction in which the iPhone is pointing.

7 Swipe up from the bottom of the screen to access options for viewing items such as gas stations and food outlets on the route. These are displayed on the map, in relation to the current route being followed

Tap once on the **End** button and then the **End Route** button to stop following the current route.

Booking a Trip

Most major travel retailers have had their own websites for a number of years. They have now moved into the world of apps, and these can be used on your iPhone to book almost any type of vacation; from cruises to city breaks.

Several apps for the iPhone (and their associated websites) offer full travel services where they can deal with flights, hotels, insurance, car hire, and excursions. These include:

- **Expedia**
- **Kayak**
- **Orbitz**
- **Travelocity**

These apps usually list special offers and last-minute deals on their Homepages, and they offer options for booking flights, hotels, car hire, and activities separately.

Hot tip

It is always worth searching different apps to get the best possible price. In some cases, it is cheapest to buy different elements of a vacation from different retailers; e.g. flights from one seller and accommodation from another.

Don't forget

Most travel apps have specific versions based on your geographical location. You will be directed to these by default.

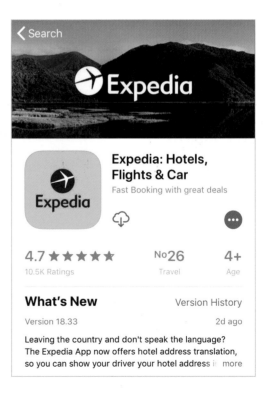

TripAdvisor

One of the best resources for travelers is TripAdvisor. Not only does the app provide a full range of opportunities for booking flights and hotels; it also has an extensive network of reviews from people who have visited the countries, hotels, and restaurants on the site. These are independent, and usually very fair and honest. In a lot of cases, if there are issues with a hotel or restaurant, the proprietor posts a reply to explain what is being done to address any problems.

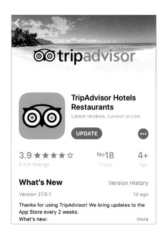

TripAdvisor has a certain sense of community, so post your own reviews once you have been places, to let others know about your experience.

165

Cruises

There are also apps dedicated specifically to cruises. One to look at is iCruise, which searches over a range of companies for your perfect cruise.

Booking Hotels

The internet is a perfect vehicle for finding good-value hotel rooms around the world. When hotels have spare capacity, this can quickly be relayed to associated websites and apps, where users can often benefit from cheap prices and special offers. There are plenty of apps that have details of thousands of hotels around the world, such as:

Trivago

An app that searches over one million hotels on more than 250 sites, to ensure you get the right hotel for the best price.

Hotels.com

A stylish app that enables you to enter search keywords into a Search box on the Home screen to find hotels based on destination, name, or local landmarks.

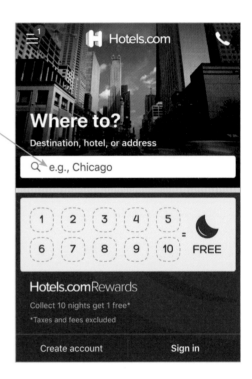

Booking.com

Another good, fully-featured hotel app that provides a comprehensive service and excellent prices.

LateRooms.com

An app that specializes in getting the best prices by dealing with rooms that are available at short notice. Some genuine bargains can be found here, for hotels of all categories.

Hot tip

Most hotel apps have reviews of all of the listed establishments. It is always worth reading these, as it gives you a view from the people who have actually been there.

Hot tip

Currency converters can also be downloaded from the App Store so that you can see how much your money is worth in different countries.

Finding Flights

Flying is a common part of modern life and although you do not have to book separate flights for a vacation (if it is part of a package), there are a number of apps for booking flights and also for following the progress of those in the air:

Skyscanner

This app can be used to find flights at airports around the world. Enter your details such as leaving airport, destination and dates of travel. The results show a range of available options, covering different price ranges and airlines.

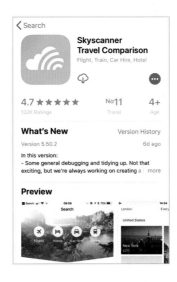

Flightradar24

If you like viewing the path of flights that are in the air, or need to check if flights are going to be delayed, this app provides this inflight information. Flights are shown according to flight number and airline.

Don't forget

Flight apps need to have an internet connection in order to show real-time flight information.

FlightAware Flight Tracker

Another app for tracking flights, showing arrivals and departures and also information about delays. It can track commercial flights worldwide.

Speaking Their Language

When you are traveling abroad, it is always beneficial to learn some of the language of the country you are visiting. With your iPhone at hand this has become a whole lot easier, and there are a number of options:

1 Translation apps that can be used to translate words, phrases and sentences in every language you probably need

Beware

Some language apps are free, but they then charge for additional content, known as "in-app purchases".

2 Language apps that offer options in several languages

3 Specific language apps, where you can fully get to grips with a new language

(11) Camera and Photos

The iPhone has a high-quality camera and the Photos app for viewing your photos.

The iPhone Camera

Because of its mobility and the quality of the screen, the iPhone is excellent for taking and displaying photos and videos. Photos can be captured directly using one of the two built-in cameras (one on the front and one on the back) and then viewed, edited, and shared using the Photos app. To do this:

1 Tap once on the **Camera** app

2 Select the Photo option and tap once on this button to capture a photo

3 Tap once on this button to swap between the front or back cameras on the iPhone

The iPhone cameras can be used for different formats. Swipe left or right just above the shutter button, to access the different shooting options:

1 Tap once on the **Square** button to capture photos at this ratio

2 Tap once on the **Video** button and press the red shutter button to take a video

3 Tap once on the **Time-lapse** button and press the shutter button (which appears in red with a ring around it) to create

a time-lapse image: the camera keeps taking photos periodically until you press the shutter button again

4 Tap once on the **Slo-Mo** button and press the red shutter button to take a slow-motion video

Don't forget

The iPhone XS and XS Max have a dual-lens camera, using a telephoto lens, and a wide-angle one for additional versatility when taking photos.

5 Tap once on the **Pano** button to create a panoramic image

6 Move the iPhone slowly to the right to create the panorama. Each photo will be taken automatically when the camera is in the correct position

7 Tap once on the **Portrait** button to capture options for portrait shots (see page 172 for details)

Hot tip

To take a quick photo, open the **Camera** app and press on either of the volume buttons.

Camera functions

The buttons at the top of the camera window can be used to create additional functionality.

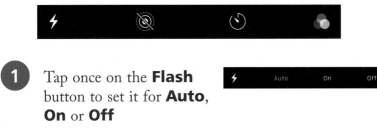

1 Tap once on the **Flash** button to set it for **Auto**, **On** or **Off**

Don't forget

Tap once on this button on the top toolbar to turn it yellow, to take a Live Photo (see page 173).

2 Tap once on the **Self-timer** button to set it for **Off**, **3s** or **10s**

3 Tap once on this button to add a filter effect before you take a photo (see page 173)

Portrait mode can be used with the both cameras on the iPhone (front-facing and back-facing). This is a new feature with iOS 12 and the latest iPhone models.

Editing depth of field in portrait photos is a new feature with iOS 12.

When creating a depth of field effect, ensure the **Portrait** button at the top of the screen is On; e.g. yellow. Tap on it once to turn it Off and edit the whole photo, not just the background.

172

...cont'd

Portrait mode
Taking photos of people is one of the most common uses for the iPhone's camera. Using the iPhone camera in Portrait it is possible to change the lighting of the photo. To do this:

 Select the **Portrait** option as shown on page 171

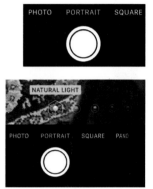

Select the lighting options are shown above the **Portrait** button. Tap once on each option to select the required mode

Adding depth of field
Portrait photos can be enhanced by blurring the background behind the subject, so that they are more prominent. This is known as "depth of field". To do this:

Open the **Photos** app and tap once on a photo taken in Portrait mode

Drag this slider to apply a blurred effect to the background of the photo. The main subject will remain unchanged

Tap once of the **Done** button to apply the depth of field effect to the photo

…cont'd

Camera filters

The camera on the iPhone can be used to apply a range of vibrant but subtle filter effects when photos are taken:

1 Tap once on the **Filters** button as shown on page 171

2 The filter effects appear at the bottom of the window. If no effect has been applied, **Original** is the selection

3 Swipe along the Filters bar to view the options. Tap once on one to apply it to the photo

Don't forget

When a filter effect has been selected, this button is displayed in the top right-hand corner of the camera window. It remains active until it is turned Off. To do this, tap once on the button to access the filters, and tap once on **Original**.

173

Live Photos

One feature on the camera is the Live Photos functionality. This enables you to take what seems like a single photo, but it creates an animated photo, which is actually a short video clip. To take Live Photos:

1 Tap once on this button on the top toolbar until it turns yellow, and **Live** appears. Take the photo using the **Photo** button, making sure that it includes some movement

2 Open the **Photos** app, and press and hold on a Live Photo to view the animated effect. The word **Live** in the top left-hand corner identifies its type

Don't forget

Swipe up on the Live Photo in the Photos app to access options for editing it. These include **Loop** and **Bounce**. Swipe from right to left to access the third option, which is **Long Exposure**.

Photo Settings

iCloud sharing

Certain photo options can be applied within Settings. Several of these are to do with storing and sharing your photos via iCloud. To access these:

1 Tap once on the **Settings** app

2 Tap once on the **Photos** tab

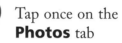

3 Drag the **iCloud Photos** button to **On** to upload your whole iPhone photo library to the iCloud. You will then be able to access this from any other Apple devices that you have. Similarly, photos on your other Apple devices can also be uploaded to the iCloud, and these will be available on your iPhone

iCloud Photos	

4 Drag the **Upload to My Photo Stream** button to **On** to enable all new photos and videos from your iPhone to be uploaded automatically to iCloud

Upload to My Photo Stream	

5 Drag the **Shared Albums** button to **On** to allow you to create albums within the Photos app that can then be shared with other people via iCloud

Shared Albums	

Drag the **Grid** button in the **Camera** settings to **On** to place a grid over the screen when you are taking photos with the camera, if required. This can be used to help compose photos by placing subjects using the grid.

Viewing Photos

Once photos have been captured, they can be viewed and organized in the Photos app. To do this:

1 Tap once on the **Photos** app

2 Tap once on the Photos button on the bottom toolbar to view photos according to when they were taken. Tap once on each window to go down to the next level

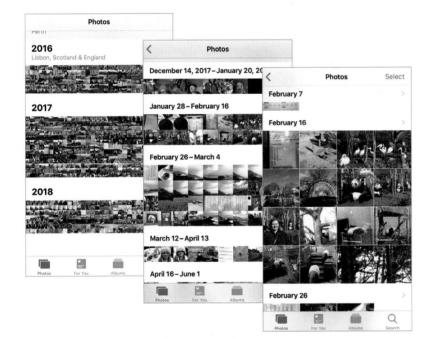

3 Tap on images to view them in more detail by date taken. Tap once on the **Back** arrow to move back a level

4 Double-tap on a photo to view it at full size, and tap once on this button to **Share** the photo

The For You tab is a new feature in the Photos app in iOS 12.

When a Memory is playing as shown in Step 4, tap once on an image on the screen and tap once on the **Edit** button in the top right-hand corner to access the editing options for the Memory. These include editing the music, title, duration, and the items in the Memory. Tap once on the **Done** button in the bottom right-hand corner to exit the editing mode.

For You Tab

In the Photos app the For You section is where the best of your photos are selected and displayed automatically. To use this:

 Tap once on the **For You** button on the bottom toolbar of the Photos app

 Memories are displayed in the **For You** section. These are collections of photos created by the Photos app, using what it determines are the best shots for a related series of photos

3 Tap once on a Memory to view its details. The top panel displays a slideshow of the photos, which are also displayed below. Tap once on the **Play** button to view a full screen slideshow of all of the images, including music

4 Albums are displayed below the Memories. These include albums that have been shared with, and by, other people

Editing Photos

The Photos app has options to perform some basic photo-editing operations. To use these:

1 Open a photo at full-screen size and tap once on the **Edit** button to access the editing tools, on the bottom toolbar

2 Tap once on the **Enhance** button to have auto-coloring editing applied to the photo

3 Tap once on the **Crop** button and drag the resizing handles to select an area of the photo that you want to keep, and click **Done** to discard the rest

4 From the Crop section, tap once on the **Rotate** button to rotate the photo 90 degrees at a time, anti-clockwise

Beware

Editing changes are made to the original photo once the changes have been saved. These will also apply to any albums into which the photo has been placed.

Don't forget

Most photos benefit from some cropping, to enhance the main subject and give it greater prominence. The Crop tool can also be used to rotate an image by degrees.

Hot tip

In the Crop section, tap once on this button to change the aspect of the photo; i.e. the dimensions at which it is displayed.

177

...cont'd

  Tap once on the **Filters** button to select special effects to be applied to the photo

Hot tip

If you reopen a photo that has been edited and closed, you have an option to **Revert** to its original state, before it was edited.

  Tap once on the **Exposure** button to enable manual color editing for different options

  For each function, tap once on the **Done** button to save the photo with the selected changes

8 Tap once on the **Cancel** button to quit the editing process

12 Practical Matters

This chapter looks at accessibility and security.

Accessibility Issues

The iPhone tries to cater to as wide a range of users as possible, including those who have difficulty with visual, hearing, or physical and motor issues. There are a number of settings that can help with these areas. To access the range of Accessibility settings:

 Tap once on the **Settings** app

 Tap once on the **General** tab

 Tap once on the **Accessibility** link

4 The settings for **Vision**, **Interaction**, **Hearing**, **Media**, and **Learning** are displayed here

You will have to scroll down the page to view the full range of Accessibility options.

Drag the **On/Off Labels** button to **On** to show the relevant icons on the On/Off buttons.

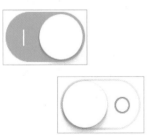

‹ General	Accessibility	
VISION		
VoiceOver	Off	›
Zoom	Off	›
Magnifier	Off	›
Display Accommodations	Off	›
Speech		›
Larger Text	Off	›
Bold Text		⬭
Button Shapes		⬭
Reduce Transparency	Off	›
Increase Contrast	Off	›
Reduce Motion	Off	›
On/Off Labels		⬭

‹ General	Accessibility	
HEARING		
MFi Hearing Devices		›
LED Flash for Alerts	Off	›
Mono Audio		⬭
Phone Noise Cancellation		⬭

Noise cancellation reduces ambient noise on phone calls when you are holding the receiver to your ear.

L   R

Adjust the audio volume balance between left and right channels.

Hearing Aid Compatibility	⬭

Hearing Aid Compatibility improves audio quality with some hearing aids.

MEDIA		
Subtitles & Captioning		›
Audio Descriptions	Off	›

Vision settings

These can help anyone with impaired vision. There are options to hear items on the screen and also for making text easier to read:

1 Tap once on the **VoiceOver** link

VoiceOver	Off >

2 Drag this button to **On** to activate the VoiceOver function. This then enables items to be spoken when you tap on them

3 Select options for VoiceOver as required, such as speaking rate and pitch

< Accessibility   **VoiceOver**

VoiceOver	⬤

VoiceOver speaks items on the screen:
- Tap once to select an item
- Double-tap to activate the selected item
- Swipe three fingers to scroll

VoiceOver Practice

SPEAKING RATE

🐢 ——————○——————— 🐇

Speech	>
Verbosity	>

4 Tap once on an item to select it (indicated by the black outline) and have it read out. Double-tap to activate a selected item or perform an action

< Accessibility   **VoiceOver**

VoiceOver	⬤

VoiceOver speaks items on the screen:
- Tap once to select an item
- Double-tap to activate the selected item
- Swipe three fingers to scroll

Beware

VoiceOver works with the pre-installed iPhone apps and some apps from the App Store, but not all of them.

Don't forget

Another useful Accessibility function is **AssistiveTouch**, within the **Interaction** section. This offers a range of options for accessing items via tapping on the screen, rather than having to use swiping with two or more fingers. Tap once on this icon to access the items within AssistiveTouch after it has been turned **On**.

...cont'd

Zoom settings

Although the iPhone screens are among the largest in the smartphone market, there are times when it can be beneficial to increase the size of the items that are being viewed. This can be done with the Zoom feature. To use this:

1 Access the Accessibility section as shown on page 180, and tap once on the Zoom link

Zoom	Off ⟩

2 By default, the **Zoom** button is **Off**

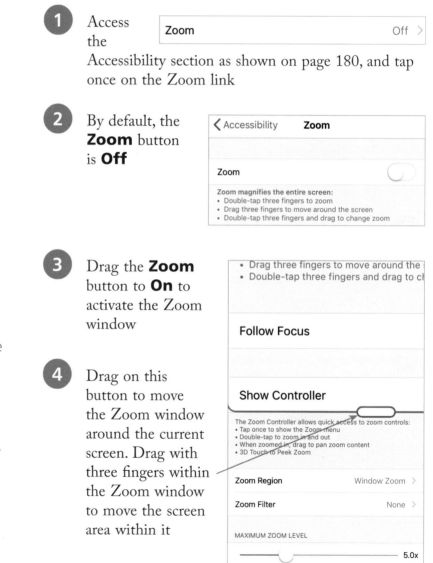

‹ Accessibility   **Zoom**

Zoom

Zoom magnifies the entire screen:
- Double-tap three fingers to zoom
- Drag three fingers to move around the screen
- Double-tap three fingers and drag to change zoom

3 Drag the **Zoom** button to **On** to activate the Zoom window

4 Drag on this button to move the Zoom window around the current screen. Drag with three fingers within the Zoom window to move the screen area within it

- Drag three fingers to move around the
- Double-tap three fingers and drag to ch

Follow Focus

Show Controller

The Zoom Controller allows quick access to zoom controls:
- Tap once to show the Zoom menu
- Double-tap to zoom in and out
- When zoomed in, drag to pan zoom content
- 3D Touch to Peek Zoom

Zoom Region	Window Zoom ⟩
Zoom Filter	None ⟩

MAXIMUM ZOOM LEVEL

5.0x

Hot tip

Drag the **Show Controller** button to **On** in the Zoom settings to display a control button for the Zoom window. Tap once on the control button to view its menu of additional features, such as zooming in to greater or lesser amounts.

5 The Zoom window can also be used on the keyboard to increase the size of the keys. As in Step 4, drag with three fingers to move to other parts of the keyboard

> **‹iCloud**   **Done**
>
> Club Champs
>
> **Men's Singles**
> John
> Nick
> Jamie
> Jeremy
> David
> Jim
>
> Q W E R T
> A S D F
> ⬆ Z X C

Text size can also be increased within the Accessibility settings. To do this:

1 Under the **Vision** section, tap once on the **Larger Text** link

> Larger Text   Off >

2 Drag the **Larger Accessibility Sizes** button **On** to enable compatible apps to show larger text sizes

> **‹Accessibility**   **Larger Text**
>
> Larger Accessibility Sizes   ⬤
>
> **Apps that support Dynamic Type will adjust to your preferred reading size below.**

3 Drag this slider to set the text size

> A   A   A

Beware

Not all apps support Dynamic Type for increasing text size, so the text in these apps will appear at their default sizes.

Finding your iPhone

No-one likes to think the worst, but if your iPhone is lost or stolen, help is at hand. The Find My iPhone function (operated through the iCloud service) allows you to locate a lost iPhone, and send a message and an alert to it. You can also remotely lock it, or even wipe its contents. This gives added peace of mind, knowing that even if your iPhone is lost or stolen, its contents will not necessarily be compromised. To set up Find My iPhone:

Hot tip

Location Services and **Find My iPhone** both have to be turned **On** to enable this service. This can be done in the Settings app (**Settings** > **Privacy** > **Location Services** > **Find iPhone**, and under **Allow Location Access** tap once on **While Using the App**).

Hot tip

If you are using Family Sharing (see pages 64-67), you can use Find Friends to locate the devices of other Family Sharing members. This can be done from your online iCloud account, or with the Find Friends app.

1 Tap once on the **Settings** app and tap once on the Apple account ID button

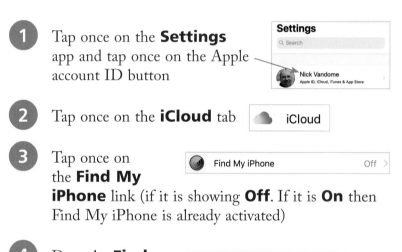

2 Tap once on the **iCloud** tab

3 Tap once on the **Find My iPhone** link (if it is showing **Off**. If it is **On** then Find My iPhone is already activated)

4 Drag the **Find My iPhone** button to **On** to be able to find your iPhone on a map

Finding a lost iPhone

Once you have set up Find My iPhone, you can search for it through the iCloud service. To do this:

1 Log in to your iCloud account at **www. icloud.com** and tap once on the **Find iPhone** button (you also have to sign in again with your Apple ID)

2 Tap once on the **All Devices** button and select your iPhone. It is identified, and its current location is displayed on the map

3 Tap once on the green circle to view details about when your iPhone was located

4 Tap once on the **Play Sound** button to send a sound alert to your iPhone

5 Tap once on the **Lost Mode** button to lock your iPhone

6 Enter a phone number where you can be contacted (optional) and tap once on the **Next** button

7 A message can also be added to be displayed on the lost iPhone. Tap once on the **Done** button to lock the iPhone. It is locked using its existing passcode, which is required to unlock it

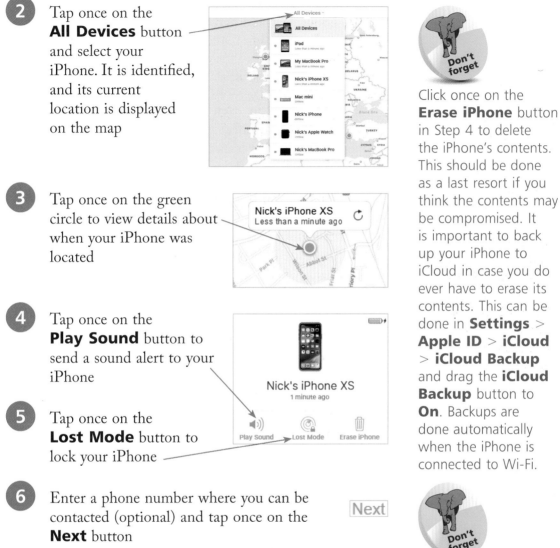

Don't forget

Click once on the **Erase iPhone** button in Step 4 to delete the iPhone's contents. This should be done as a last resort if you think the contents may be compromised. It is important to back up your iPhone to iCloud in case you do ever have to erase its contents. This can be done in **Settings** > **Apple ID** > **iCloud** > **iCloud Backup** and drag the **iCloud Backup** button to **On**. Backups are done automatically when the iPhone is connected to Wi-Fi.

Don't forget

If you have Apple Pay set up on your iPhone, this will be suspended if Lost Mode is enabled. It will be reactivated when the passcode is entered to unlock it and your Apple ID entered within Settings.

Don't forget

Malware is short for malicious software, designed to harm your iPhone or access and distribute information from it.

Don't forget

Apple also checks apps that are provided through the App Store, and this process is very robust. This does not mean that it is impossible for a virus to infect the iPhone, so keep an eye on the Apple website to see if there are any details about iPhone viruses.

Avoiding Viruses

As far as security from viruses on the iPhone is concerned, there is good news and bad news:

- The good news is that, due to its architecture, most apps on the iPhone do not communicate with each other unless specifically required to, such as the Mail and the Contacts apps. So, even if there were a virus, it would be difficult for it to infect the whole iPhone. Also, Apple performs rigorous tests on apps that are submitted to the App Store (although even this is not foolproof; see next bullet point).

- The bad news is that no computer system is immune from viruses and malware, and complacency is one of the biggest enemies of computer security. The iPhone's popularity means it is an attractive target for hackers and virus writers. There have been instances of photos in iCloud being accessed and hacked, but this was more to do with password security, or lack of, than viruses. There have also been some, rare, malicious attacks centered around the code used to create apps for the App Store. In some cases, certain apps were affected before the virus was located and remedial action taken. This is a reminder of the need for extreme vigilance against viruses, and for users to check in the media for information about any new attacks. Search the web for "latest viruses" to find websites that specialize in identifying the latest software viruses and threats.

Antivirus options

There are a few apps in the App Store that deal with antivirus issues, although not actually removing viruses. Two options to look at are:

- **McAfee** apps. The online security firm has a number of apps that cover issues such as privacy and passwords.

- **Norton** apps. Similar to McAfee, Norton offers a range of security apps for the iPhone.

Index

187

G

H

I

K